D0984455

INCREASING ALPHA WITH OPTIONS

INCREASING ALPHA WITH OPTIONS

Trading Strategies Using Technical
Analysis and Market Indicators

SCOTT H. FULLMAN, CMT

BLOOMBERG PRESS
An Imprint of
WILEY

Technical analysis involves learning from history and experience in order to project into the future. I therefore dedicate this book to the late William H. Fullman, Jr., Sandie Fullman, James Boyd Taylor, and Doris J. Taylor, who my wife and I have learned countless lessons from, and to our children Jonathan William Fullman and Daniel Scott Fullman, who we have taught and loved using those life experiences.

Contents

Acknowledgments

My wife, Deborah, her understanding with the time consuming writing and editing deadlines.

Michael Ham, a colleague that has taught me much and who reviewed my work and been there to bounce questions off of.

Ingrid Case, who edited the book and made insightful changes and suggestions.

Steven Isaacs, project manager at Bloomberg Press, for all of his help in producing this work.

The CEOs of WJB Capital Group, Craig Rothfeld and Michael Romano, for their support in both writing this book and the work I do for the firm and its clients each and every day.

Adam Futterman, head of derivatives trading, and the derivatives trading team at WJB Capital Group for their insight on what clients are looking for today.

John Roque and Adolfo Rueda, our technical team, for their insights and inspiration.

My colleagues at WJB Capital for all of their efforts and conversations that led me to the decision to write this book.

John and Debbie Cirenza, Ray Dempsey, Michael Eisenberg, and Carl Romick for their never ending input on the trading pits.

My friends and associates at the Market Technicians Association (MTA), with whom I frequently consult in respect to the markets and forms of analysis.

My many friends, colleagues, and associates at the options exchanges and in the industry, whom I have learned a lot from and shared ideas with over the years.

Introduction

WELCOME TO THE world of twenty-first–century investing, a world of intertwined derivative products, analysis methods, and global markets in which countries' politics, currencies, debt, and equities all interact.

In this new world of investing, managers deal with a variety of dynamics, products, analyses, and risk controls. As ever, professional managers concern themselves with resource availability and cost as they chase above-benchmark performance and profits—called *alpha*—and compete against other managers for new investment dollars. Many investment managers focus on performance during most of their waking hours.

In doing so, they seek to balance risk against the possibility of reward. Investment managers have always done this, of course, but the job grew more complicated during the 1990s, when hedge funds and mutual funds grew increasingly popular. The latter part of the decade, particularly in the United States, was characterized by impressive market performance, the result of growth in technology and the Internet, as well as financial service sector expansion. Hedge and mutual funds paid top managers attractive compensation, which helped increase both the number of funds and the competition among them.

Hedge and mutual funds examined every aspect of their businesses, trying to maximize growth and performance. Many developed new techniques. Some of these resulted from new products, such as exchange-traded funds (ETF). Others came from new analysis applications, such as pair trades that are derived from quantitative comparisons of two or more companies within the same group. Fund managers expanded the ways they used arbitrage, short selling, and other traditional strategies.

More and more funds were managed from the United States and Europe, though many were registered in other countries, allowing managers to attract more money from overseas and pay lower taxes.

The best-performing funds attracted more capital than their competition, boosting managers' compensation even higher. Chasing ever-better returns, some fund managers deviated from their normal practices and directives, overleveraging and taking on extra risk. Sometimes that risk was excessive or highly concentrated in a single market, sector, industry group, or security.

Markets collapsed from the subprime mortgage crisis, which resulted in a sharp sell-off and contraction in the credit markets. Most funds lost money; those that were overleveraged and had taken on additional risk often lost more than did their more conservative fellows. Some went out of business, while others faced dwindling client bases.

Derivatives strategists—including me—learned a lot from this period. Strategists saw that new strategies—and new uses of older strategies—can help investors generate better profits at lower risk levels. In this book, I will examine useful analytical techniques, showing readers how to create alpha—profits—while also protecting positions from adverse market changes.

The Prime Directive

Star Trek fans may remember the "prime directive," the most important rule for anyone in Star Fleet Command. It stated, "No one shall interfere in the governance and development of life on other planets." Starship captains and crews would sacrifice their own lives to obey the prime directive.

In investment management, protecting capital and assets should be the prime directive. People entrust managers with their money in amounts that—whether they seem large or small to the manager—are significant to asset owners, who worked hard to earn them. From competing choices, asset holders choose managers in whom they have some confidence, basing their selections on factors that include track record, education, references, and experience. Investment managers should take clients' trust very seriously, carefully considering their mandates and investment positions—and the potential for quick changes in market conditions.

Capital preservation is good for clients, but it's also good for managers. Strategies that preserve capital before pursuing profit may encourage clients to keep money in a fund during a downturn and can offer better profits in a rough market than can more risk-oriented tactics. Defensive strategies and reduced losses may also attract capital away from competing funds as investors review performance.

Why Technical Analysis?

Technical analysis, I believe, can help investment managers effectively pursue the twin goals of capital preservation and profit.

Many people have asked me why I pursue technical analysis, rather than fundamental analysis. In truth, I consider both. I look at the impact of news—especially fundamental news—on a company or other financial instrument, particularly noting instances when a particular piece of news does not have the expected effect. I look at unusual trading, looking for the increased volume or price movements that can be a sign of new accumulation or distribution. I also monitor the listed derivatives markets for unusual trading.

I focus on technical analysis, however, because profits and losses happen on Wall Street—not at a company's headquarters. I'm more concerned with a stock's movements than with underlying company fundamentals. What's more, technical trends often change well before fundamental shifts begin to show. This is especially true for equities.

June 2007 offers an example of this phenomenon. The financial sector led a bull market that lasted from March 2003 to October 2007. Financial company shares generally peaked in June. The stocks that led the market higher, however, peaked nearly five months before the major benchmarks set their cycle highs. Financial stocks' downturn also occurred as the companies continued to report growth, increased earnings, and other good news.

Consider the case of Citigroup (NYSE: C). One of the largest and most diverse financial services companies and banks in the world, Citibank offers institutional and retail banking, investment services, investment banking, and credit products from offices all over the world.

Figure I.1 A weekly chart on Citigroup. Note how the stock broke the supporting trend line in mid-July, the first warning signal that something was wrong.

Figure I.1 shows that Citigroup shares began to turn lower in July 2007, even as the company announced global operations expansion and strong earnings. Technical analysis showed that the company had broken a three-year supporting trend line, offering the first signal that something was wrong. A supporting trend line connects a trend's low points.

Several months later, the company began to report problems. The first involved the declining value of residential mortgages, particularly within Citigroup's subprime loan portfolio. As borrowers defaulted on those loans, Citigroup's stock suffered. Ripple effects hurt the financial services sector, and ultimately the entire world economy.

American casualties included Lehman Brothers (NYSE: LEH), Bear Stearns (NYSE: BSC), and American International Group (NYSE: AIG). Nearly all financial institutions felt the pain, as did businesses related to real estate. Eventually, of course, the contagion spread to businesses and economies around the globe.

Technical Analysis and Time Management

I have additional reasons, both practical and philosophical, for appreciating technical analysis. I am both a strategist and a Chartered Market

Technician (CMT): a technical analyst who has passed a series of qualifying examinations from the Market Technicians Association (MTA).

I do a lot of customized programming, for clients as well as myself, and create proprietary analytical tools that monitor global markets, sectors, industry groups, ETFs, individual stocks, commodities, currencies, and other instruments. I focus on U.S. markets, but still search globally for relationships that may signal Wall Street's next move. My data may not include every single market or instrument, but I'm still monitoring an extremely large number of instruments. There are not enough hours in the week to use fundamental analysis on each one.

Technical analysis, by contrast, makes it humanly possible to keep track of all these instruments. In about an hour and a half each week I get a general idea of which markets are performing well, which are leading or laggards, and what general trends I might expect.

Next, I look at the major currencies and their interactions—particularly when those interactions involve the U.S. dollar. The relationship between the British pound and Japanese yen can also be very interesting, showing import and export trends and sometimes explaining other market movements.

I move on to the commodities markets, which can sometimes shed light on countrywide market movements—which in turn affect sectors, industry groups, and individual stocks. At times, stocks or sectors in a particular commodities market move before analysts see changes in the market as a whole. Known as an instance of the tail wagging the dog, this phenomenon can form the basis for profitable trades.

Then I consider sectors and industry groups, using different forms *crucial* of analysis to look at momentum, relative performance, money flow, and other factors that can identify leaders, laggards, and trend changes. I focus on currently important groups, identifying individual stocks within those groups and trading those that are having the biggest impact.

To focus on the U.S. markets—the world's largest markets by country— I spend about five hours reviewing technical charts for the best buy and sell opportunities. In that time, I may identify continuing trends, stagnant formations, and trend changes. Once a week I look at daily charts on nearly 3,000 issues; twice a month (or more, depending on market activity) I look at weekly charts on the same issues; once a quarter I look at monthly charts.

I also consider individual stocks' perceived risk, as measured using options' implied volatility readings and the implied volatility of relevant market benchmarks. I often use the CBOE S&P 500 Implied Volatility Index, also known as VIX, and sometimes referred to as the "fear gauge."

The VIX measures implied volatility by reversing an options valuation formula, such as the Black-Scholes options pricing model, and using an option's current price to solve for the volatility level that the current option value implies. When individual options have different risk premiums, traders can average or index implied risk figures to determine the stock's implied risk. High risk typically goes hand in hand with high options premiums, and thus with high implied volatility readings.

Options professionals typically sell higher premiums or volatility, a strategy known as "selling gamma." When premiums are low, professionals purchase options, a strategy known as "buying gamma."

When risk perceptions are low, as they were in 2005–2006, implied volatility levels are generally low. Conversely, when risk perceptions are high, as they were in 2008, implied volatility levels are generally high. Figure I.2 is a weekly VIX chart showing changes in implied volatility

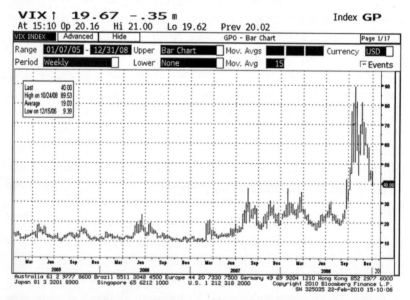

Figure I.2 A weekly chart on the CBOE S&P 500 Implied Volatility Index (VIX). Notice the sharp increase in this indicator as the market adjusted risk valuations during the late third-quarter and early fourth-quarter of 2008.

between 2005 and 2006, when implied volatility levels were generally low, and in 2008, when risk perceptions were high. Note that the VIX implied volatility dropped below 10 percent in 2006 (A), a historically low reading. VIX rose to a historic high (B) of 89.53 percent, an indication that premiums were extremely high.

Because the VIX is an index based on S&P 500 stock options, its reading may be lower than that of many of its component issues. An index might move 10 percent in a single day, in extreme cases. On that same day, one or more of the same index's component issues may have moved by more than 20 percent, and even above 50 percent. There is a low probability that more than half the index's components will reach extreme thresholds, but there is a higher probability that more than half the index's components will exceed the index itself.

Strategies

I use all this information to create strategies. These are based not only on price targets and anticipated movements, but also on market risk, volatility, trading environment, and investors' risk/reward profiles. In many cases my published ideas may not meet clients' risk/reward profiles, so I look for other strategies that do meet their profiles.

Maximizing Profit, Minimizing Risk

Investment managers often worry about losing potential investors to better-performing competitors. There are flexible ways to improve performance without necessarily incurring more risk. The techniques outlined in the chapters ahead will help reduce the frustration and confusion you might feel about those techniques, helping you take the best advantage of all of the tools at your disposal.

INCREASING ALPHA WITH OPTIONS

CHAPTER 1

Why Technical Analysis?

IF YOU'VE PICKED UP this book, you're probably at least interested in technical analysis, but perhaps you're not fully convinced that technical analysis should be part of your management plan. Maybe it's not your cup of coffee, or maybe it's just not in your fund's mandate. That's okay. Most funds have fundamentally based analysis and may be slow to accept charting as a valid research tool, or options as valid investments. But every time a strong bear market or significant correction appears—accompanied by a volatility spike—more managers and funds begin to at least consider options and chart patterns.

Stocks tend to move ahead of fundamentals; corporate information and data can be as much as six months behind share movement. By acting on information gained through technical analysis, managers can sometimes prevent a fund from losing profits and/or capital. That's a compelling argument for technical analysis, even for fundamentalists.

Fundamental analysis considers companies in many different ways: Outlook and business operations, balance sheet and income statement, competitive factors, and other variables help analysts create fair market valuations and price targets for underlying shares. Analysts closely monitor the effect of news and other events on a company, but they generally form expectations for periods that exceed nine months and are sometimes as long as 18 months to two years. By the time fundamentals have run their projected or extended courses, share prices may have peaked or turned lower. (In many cases, investors see this as a buying opportunity, which may create a bounce.) Technical analysis can help you predict movements during those projection periods.

If you cannot or will not use technical analysis to make trading decisions, you may at least want to use technical analysis to warn you of potential changes to fundamentals before they happen. Consider using and monitoring monthly charts, and consulting the weekly charts if you see a significant price change.

Consider some examples of how and why this works. Technical analysis works well in part because stock trading is tied to economic factors and cycles, with sectors and industry groups moving higher and lower based on their places in the cycle.

As cycles and economics play out, insiders buy and sell shares in response to changing business expectations. Insiders—everyone from the CEO to a guy on the loading dock—are often good at spotting the factors that affect the company's bottom line. Some of these individuals may not be allowed to trade company stock; others (such as the guy on the loading dock) may not be required to report trades to the Securities and Exchange Commission (SEC), so their transactions go unnoticed.

But officers and other qualified insiders can trade their own companies' stock and must tell the SEC when they do. They notify the SEC—and, through them, the rest of the financial world—through Form 4 filings. In Figure 1.1 we see that seven insiders sold 35,846 shares of stock on June 8. The insiders bought many of those shares by exercising corporate options days earlier.

SEC filings reveal insider trading. Share movements—in both price and volume—show what the so-called smart money is doing. Smart money, in this context, belongs to people who have a close company association. They may be suppliers, customers, partners, service providers, or others with knowledge and opportunities for close observance.

Share movement generally gets the attention of astute investors, managers, and technicians. Price breakouts and other factors associated with stock accumulation often attract new buyers and may bring the first technical signal that the stock is breaking out. As more investors and analysts begin to notice share movement, buying pressure will likely increase, providing the breakout.

Low valuations are common when a stock is beginning to take off. Real and estimated price/earnings ratios and price-to-book readings will also be low, attracting value investors and managers. These leaders usually help attract other buyers.

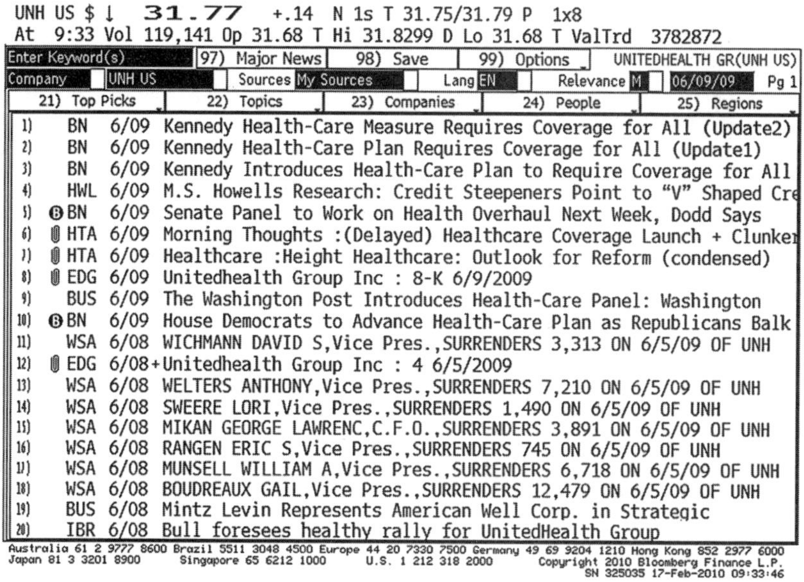

```
UNH US $ ↓  31.77   +.14  N 1s T 31.75/31.79 P  1x8
At   9:33 Vol 119,141 Op 31.68 T Hi 31.8299 D Lo 31.68 T ValTrd  3782872
Enter Keyword(s)        97) Major News   98) Save    99) Options    UNITEDHEALTH GR(UNH US)
Company     UNH US       Sources My Sources    Lang EN      Relevance M   06/09/09   Pg 1
  21)  Top Picks        22) Topics      23) Companies     24) People      25) Regions
 1)    BN   6/09  Kennedy Health-Care Measure Requires Coverage for All (Update2)
 2)    BN   6/09  Kennedy Health-Care Plan Requires Coverage for All (Update1)
 3)    BN   6/09  Kennedy Introduces Health-Care Plan to Require Coverage for All
 4)    HWL  6/09  M.S. Howells Research: Credit Steepeners Point to "V" Shaped Cre
 5) ⊕ BN   6/09  Senate Panel to Work on Health Overhaul Next Week, Dodd Says
 6) ▯ HTA  6/09  Morning Thoughts :(Delayed) Healthcare Coverage Launch + Clunker
 7) ▯ HTA  6/09  Healthcare :Height Healthcare: Outlook for Reform (condensed)
 8) ▯ EDG  6/09  Unitedhealth Group Inc : 8-K 6/9/2009
 9)    BUS  6/09  The Washington Post Introduces Health-Care Panel: Washington
10) ⊕ BN   6/09  House Democrats to Advance Health-Care Plan as Republicans Balk
11)    WSA  6/08  WICHMANN DAVID S,Vice Pres.,SURRENDERS 3,313 ON 6/5/09 OF UNH
12) ▯ EDG  6/08+ Unitedhealth Group Inc : 4 6/5/2009
13)    WSA  6/08  WELTERS ANTHONY,Vice Pres.,SURRENDERS 7,210 ON 6/5/09 OF UNH
14)    WSA  6/08  SWEERE LORI,Vice Pres.,SURRENDERS 1,490 ON 6/5/09 OF UNH
15)    WSA  6/08  MIKAN GEORGE LAWRENC,C.F.O.,SURRENDERS 3,891 ON 6/5/09 OF UNH
16)    WSA  6/08  RANGEN ERIC S,Vice Pres.,SURRENDERS 745 ON 6/5/09 OF UNH
17)    WSA  6/08  MUNSELL WILLIAM A,Vice Pres.,SURRENDERS 6,718 ON 6/5/09 OF UNH
18)    WSA  6/08  BOUDREAUX GAIL,Vice Pres.,SURRENDERS 12,479 ON 6/5/09 OF UNH
19)    BUS  6/08  Mintz Levin Represents American Well Corp. in Strategic
20)    IBR  6/08  Bull foresees healthy rally for UnitedHealth Group
Australia 61 2 9777 8600 Brazil 5511 3048 4500 Europe 44 20 7330 7500 Germany 49 69 9204 1210 Hong Kong 852 2977 6000
Japan 81 3 3201 8900    Singapore 65 6212 1000    U.S. 1 212 318 2000    Copyright 2010 Bloomberg Finance L.P.
                                                              SN 325035 17-Feb-2010 09:33:46
```

Figure 1.1 This Bloomberg Professional news screen shows the sales of UNH shares being filed with the SEC on June 8.

Most of the buyers that enter the market at this point are not looking to make a quick profit. They are long-term investors who expect a target company's business to grow. They monitor business activity, looking for improvements and checking whether or not their investments stay on track.

Bases

After a company goes through a decline, shares typically go into a low-volatility, sideways trend that's called a base. Trend character-istics include contracting Bollinger Band lines and a low Average Directional Momentum Index (ADX) reading. Share prices may be relatively low compared to the past year or two. Look for basing on a weekly chart rather than a daily chart, because a daily chart's period may not be long enough to show a real base, one that will support a share breakout.

Bases don't always happen, but they're easy to identify and offer use-ful information, particularly when they last at least one quarter. That happened for Apple Inc. (AAPL), shown in Figure 1.2. Note the stock's sideways movement between October and March on the weekly chart,

Figure 1.2 This Bloomberg Professional chart of Apple Inc. (AAPL) shows the weekly movement and the base that formed between October and March.

a pattern accompanied by waning volume. Measure upward from the base along the x-axis to project a target stock price. The longer the base, the greater the shares' upward potential.

Figure 1.3 shows AAPL after the breakout. Our initial measurement showed that the stock should move to around $150 from $101. The stock hit that target nearly three months after the breakout for a gain of nearly 45 percent.

Volatility continued to contract as the base formed, declining on both an implied (based on option premiums) and a historic (based on share movement) basis. Figure 1.4 shows the continuous decline in volatility, even after the stock broke out and rose from the base. (This is a daily chart, not a weekly chart, so we are not showing an apples-to-apples comparison between stock price and volatility.)

The low volatility level indicates that option premiums (and risk perceptions) were comparatively low, which provides an opportunity for would-be investors. Because these investments are generally longer-term, an investor can use the Long-tErm AnticiPation Securities (LEAPS™) as an alternative to purchasing shares. LEAPS are long-term options, initially listed for trading with about 30 months of life until expiration.

Figure 1.3 Bloomberg Professional chart on Apple Inc. (AAPL) after the breakout. Note how the stock was just below the $150 initial target price!

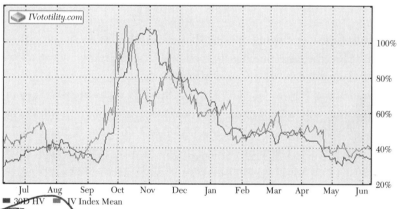

Figure 1.4 30-day historic and implied volatility chart on Apple Inc. (AAPL), courtesy of iVolatility.com.

utmost
crucial

Unlike regular options, these contracts are only on select stocks with higher levels of trading activity, interest, and liquidity.

Advantages include the ability to leverage an investment by putting up less initial capital. Risks include a potential total loss of capital—but this is less than the cost of buying the shares in either a cash or margin

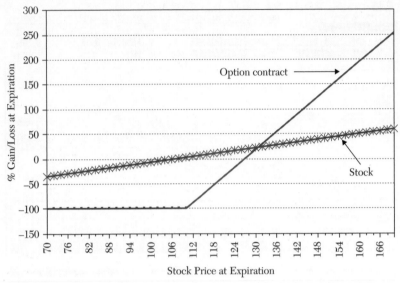

Figure 1.5 Payoff chart for Apple Inc. comparing the stock vs. the purchase of the long-term call option. Returns are based on intrinsic price at expiration. Time premium would likely add additional profit and percentage return prior to expiration.

account. Consider buying options that are equivalent to the stock you might otherwise have purchased, then investing the remainder in a low-risk instrument, such as a Treasury bond.

As shown in Figure 1.5, AAPL was at $106.85 as the breakout began. A call option with a $110 strike price and nearly nine months until expiration cost $17. When the stock reached $146.40 on June 8, that option's price was $39.20. The unrealized gain was $22.20 per share, or 130.6 percent, compared to a potential gain of $39.55 per share, or 37 percent. Notice that the leveraged option return was nearly 3 1/2 times that of the stock. These returns don't include the approximate 2 percent gain from owning Treasury securities.

Fundamentals vs. Technicals

For value investors, technical analysis may have helped confirm expectations that business conditions would improve. Insiders and those in the know began to accumulate stock with the expectation that business would improve later in the year.

The base's beginning shows that insiders bought 22,359 company shares in two transactions. Several weeks later insiders sold small share blocks, then bought another 33,296 shares in late January. After the breakout insiders bought another 1,204 shares, and one insider sold nearly 8,000 shares.

One might say that we missed the bottom by waiting for the breakout—but we weren't trying to find the bottom. It's impossible to consistently find stock price bottoms, and doing so may mean tying up capital in positions that resolve slowly. By giving up a small amount of profit potential, we raise the probability of making a correct investment decision.

almost crucial

As I noted earlier, basing patterns are usually most effective when they take several months to form. Growth over one or two quarters provides a nice base and plenty of upside potential. The longer the base, the greater the shares' potential upward movement. However, investors who own positions during the basing period commit capital and may sacrifice other opportunities, especially if shares remain stagnant for an extended period of time. A stock's sideways trend might last for more than a year, giving market underperformance in a bull market and sometimes even in a bear market. Such trends contribute little to fund performance or investor loyalty.

Investors who buy long calls on a breakout see varying times to profitability. In some patterns a decline to the breakout point may follow the breakout; the market tests that price point before the positive trend resumes. This is a new buying opportunity for those that missed the breakout, or for those who bought partial positions. Once the positive trend resumes, the pattern confirms that the breakout was not a false event. Exit the position if the breakout point is violated and shares go back into the sideways trend pattern or (worse) break the support.

A positive breakout affirmation should bring positive news from the company—if not immediately, then in the near future. This should increase trend momentum. A failed breakout suggests that fundamental analysts should look for reasons that the stock is failing. If the stock continues to move lower on positive news, something is wrong.

Maintaining the long call position is important. Doing so lowers the position's risk and helps maintain market interest, and therefore liquidity. Generally, however, investors take action on a stock position that moves higher by at least 10 percent. In this situation a manager might sell the long call and roll it into another long call in the same expiration month, but at a higher strike price. The premium is less tied to the sold contract's economic value, so the move typically takes out most of the initial capital and some profit, leaving a position with reduced capital exposure.

A manager might also sell an out-of-the-money call option with a closer expiration date, especially if the implied volatility level has risen and the skew shows higher implied volatility on shorter-term than longer-term contracts. This would limit the potential upside, but the premium received by writing these calls would increase profits if upward movement stalls, or if the stock goes into a corrective or consolidation phase.

Tops

Absolutely crucial

Sideways patterns are also possible at tops, although they are less frequent and usually shorter. Implied volatility levels are usually relatively low at tops, because investors may feel complacent following share appreciation. Most investors are slow to sell a stock. They hope shares will continue to rise, and they often feel loyalty toward the company and its shares, especially after a significant gain. When the stock does begin a descent, investors may think the decline is just a correction to the advance and believe that the upward trend will likely resume in the near future.

Tops often involve or anticipate real-time events: a slowdown in orders, higher resource prices, contract loss, and competitive pressures. A health care company, for instance, might face the loss of patent protection for a key product. Decreasing margins, stronger competition, and lower profits will all put the company's future under pressure.

Figure 1.6 is a daily chart on Johnson & Johnson from June 12, 2006 to January 26, 2007. The stock was at a high of $69.41 on October 23 and then set a marginally lower high on November 7 at $69.03. An apparent correction/consolidation pattern developed and lasted from mid-October into mid-January, a three-month period.

Figure 1.7 shows that shares complete a short-term head-and-shoulders top, but find support at the consolidation support line. The stock breaks support on February 21, sending shares back toward the June 2006 lows. Volume increases during the decline as momentum increases.

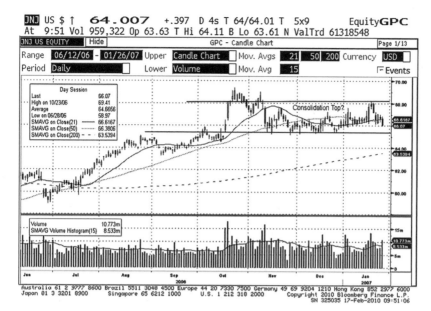

Figure 1.6 Bloomberg Professional chart on Johnson & Johnson (JNJ)—Daily chart from June 12, 2006 to January 26, 2007. Notice the consolidation that formed between November and January. There was even a very short-term head-and-shoulders top that formed toward the end of the consolidation.

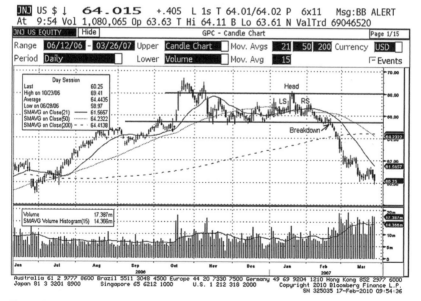

Figure 1.7 Bloomberg Professional chart on Johnson & Johnson (JNJ)—Daily chart from June 12, 2006 to March 26, 2007. Notice the break in the consolidation following a head-and-shoulders top pattern. Volume increased on the breakdown.

utmost! crucial

Implied volatility declined to a low of 10.27 percent—its lowest level in years—before the February 21 breakdown. As the shares broke support, volatility rose to a high of 16.08 percent on March 13. Shares bounced and dropped back to a higher low, but implied volatility didn't retrace to its lows. (It did narrow the space between highs and lows.)

Using long-term options with fundamental analysis works in bearish and bullish scenarios. Investors who use options instead of selling shares short don't have to borrow the shares, pay a rebate, be bought in, or be squeezed if a positive trend resumes. Alternatively, long-term puts may be an attractive purchase for managers who believe that shares may decline in the intermediate to long term. By purchasing a put contract just as the shares break consolidation support, investors get the best opportunity for both timing and pricing. Puts typically cost less when implied volatility levels are near their lows, and would-be short-sellers avoid holding a short position for what might be a long time as they wait for the breakdown.

utmost crucial

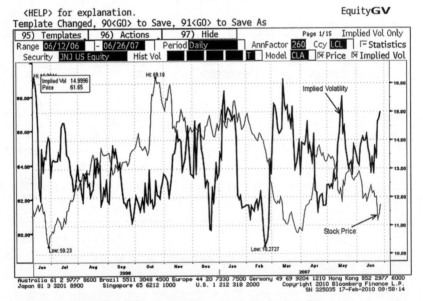

Figure 1.8 Bloomberg Professional chart showing the closing price of the stock and implied volatility on Johnson & Johnson (JNJ) during the period between June 2006 and June 2007.

My arguments for using technical analysis aren't intended to imply that fundamentals don't count. They absolutely do. Technical analysis, however, can offer useful insights at times when a stock is moving in one direction and company expectations are moving in another. It can quickly and efficiently reveal shorter-term events and trends that affect a company's stock and can also offer a time-efficient and economical alternative to primary fundamental research, which typically costs a great deal of time and money—particularly when it's done well. Pair technical analysis with fundamental analysis, by contrast, and you'll get the most for your money, uncovering trends, problems, and opportunities that you might not otherwise see.

CHAPTER 2

The Basics of Technical Analysis

TO UNDERSTAND TECHNICAL ANALYSIS, one must first understand the varying elements of this analysis system: chart type, analysis period, and time itself. Some of these are more important than others, depending on the chart type and discipline an analyst uses. Some technical indicators, such as oscillators, may be available on some charts but not on others.

Understanding Chart Types

The most basic chart type is the line chart. Line charts simply connect one period's closing prices to those of another period, covering an hour, a day, a week, a quarter, or even a year. Line chart construction is simple and allows the user to eliminate trading noise and concentrate on the last price, which is the most important price of any period. (I define random market movements, especially when accompanied by low volume levels, as marketplace noise. For most securities, the opening, high, low, and closing prices, plus volume, are the important numbers. Most managers will find that they waste resources by analyzing every small trade.)

Line charts do have a disadvantage: They don't show price movement beyond the last price value. (Other formations, by contrast, show price movement within a given period's ranges and boundaries.) Analysts using a line chart may have difficulty determining the time period's support and resistance points, which may have kept share prices from further movement. Line charts also remove most of the visual impact that volatility creates.

Another type of chart, the bar chart, is probably the most popular technical analysis chart type. Analysts construct bar charts by drawing horizontal lines that represent a stock's high and low ranges during the measurement period. A tick to the right of the chart shows the closing value; an optional tick to the left shows the opening value. (Not all bar charts show the opening value.)

Bar charts have several advantages. They include the range of trades during the measurement period and let analysts see the ranges' boundaries. It's easier to identify support and resistance levels on bar charts than on line charts. A disadvantage of bar charts, however, is that they may include market noise and irrelevant outliers, which can cloud an analyst's view.

My favorite chart type, Japanese candlesticks, combines the best features of line and bar charts. Candlestick charts show price ranges and illustrate the relationship between opening and closing values. The "body" of a candlestick data point shows the difference between opening and closing values. Vertical lines, called "shadows," stretch between the candles' tops and bottoms to indicate upper and lower values. The body is not colored or is colored white (some systems use green) when the opening value is below the closing value. When the closing value is below the opening value, the body is colored dark or black (some systems use red).

Figure 2.1 compares line, bar, and Japanese candlestick charts, all of which can offer intraday, daily, weekly, monthly, or annual performance data. These different views can help illustrate short-term, intermediate-term, long-term, and very long-term trends.

Notice the different levels of detail and information. In my opinion, the Japanese candlestick chart provides the greatest detail, as well as the best illustration of support and resistance levels, compared to the previous two chart styles.

The candlesticks themselves also provide a great deal of information. Candlesticks have been used in various markets, including raw commodities markets, for hundreds of years. The Japanese believe that the difference between the opening and closing price shows important pressures between bulls and bears, a source of potential signals.

Point and figure is another popular chart type. Point and figure charts are based strictly on price movements and price movement reversals, with positive movements represented by a series of Xs and negative

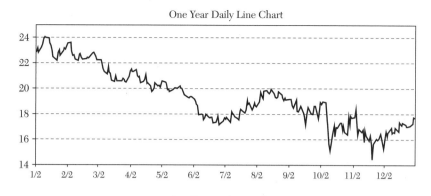

One Year Daily Line Chart

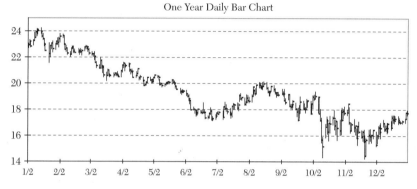

One Year Daily Bar Chart

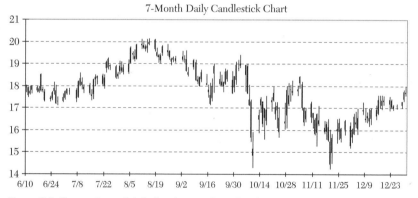

7-Month Daily Candlestick Chart

Figure 2.1 Comparison of daily line, bar, and candlestick charts on Pfizer (PFE).

movements by a series of Os. Time is *not* a dimension in a point and figure chart and does not affect the chart's analytical value.

Point and figure charts offer a clear view of trends. Their lack of a time dimension, however, makes it difficult to use them in creating strategies, especially short- and intermediate-term strategies. Strategies are

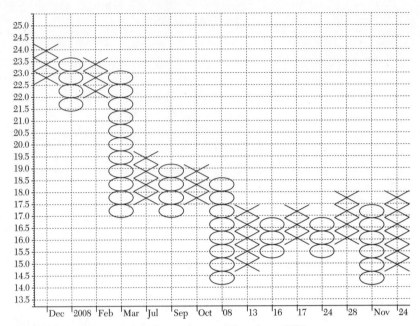

Figure 2.2 One-year point and figure chart on Pfizer Corp. (PFE).

based on options contracts, which have an expiration date. Figure 2.2 shows the same data as Figure 2.1, expressed using point and figure analysis.

Trend Properties

To understand trends and countertrends, you'll need a feel for their basic characteristics. This will also help you create strategies for various trend conditions.

Bull trends tend to last longer than bear trends and often show rising volume as they progress. When the greatest numbers of investors are bullish, the bull trend may be nearing its end. That positive sentiment usually occurs when nearly every investor has a long position commitment, so this can be a good time to hedge those positions.

Positive trends often feature a contraction in option risk premiums, because implied volatility levels and risk perception normally decline together, and because upward markets are often smoother than their negative counterparts. Premium contractions may draw more buyers to purchase options, rather than stock. Options may look like the more

utmost

crucial

economical choice, especially as stock prices are much higher than when the trend started.

Call volume may also rise for another reason: leverage. Buying call contracts lets investors realize greater percentage increases compared with absolute dollar gains, in more diversified portfolios, than if they had invested the same money in stock.

During bull markets, analysts may race to upgrade their opinions and target prices. Even weak stocks may ride this wave, which usually occurs during periods of economic expansion.

Bull markets (and bear market rallies) also attract buyers to broad-based exchange-traded funds (ETFs). These funds let buyers minimize their exposures by diversifying. Purchasing contracts, such as the S&P Depository Trust (SPY), allows for SPX performance, which is usually lower but safer than buying every share in SPY or even a representative group of SPX shares.

Negative trends are often sharp, quick, and volatile. Their movements are usually exaggerated, compared to the previous bull trend. Volume is usually high on extreme downward movement days, but may be lower overall than volume in positive trends. Investors tend to sell slowly during a negative trend, but selling often accelerates if panic begins to dominate the market. As the market declines, investors feel an increasing urgency to close positions, minimize exposure, and contain risk, especially as benchmarks break through key support levels and psychologically important numbers.

Companies may cut or eliminate dividends, especially when the negative trend continues and the economy is contracting. Boards of directors at many companies move to preserve capital, especially when business activity is slowing. Companies may be slow to resume paying stock dividends, as the board awaits evidence of a market and economic recovery.

During these declines, investors may see sharp increases in option premiums as risk perception increases. Even during small countertrend rallies, volatility levels may remain elevated. Option premiums rose to extreme levels during past major bear markets, such as the crash of 1987, the mini-crash of 1989, downward movement following the terrorist attacks of 1993 and 2001, and the market crash of 2008. At several points during the 2008–2009 market crash, volatility rose so high that it effectively shut down the options markets and had a significant impact on the equities markets.

During such markets, managers who must be fully invested may reallocate capital investments into defensive sectors and stocks. These stocks usually fall at a slower rate than do growth stocks.

Put activity generally rises, even when premiums are also increasing. Writing call options, though attractive during periods of increased volatility, is inherently risky. Many fund managers are not allowed to sell naked call options, because of the increased risk of a short-stock squeeze and attendant volatility.

When investors jump into put or call option contracts, volume on one option type usually rises; the other may or may not change. When share prices decline sharply, however, we usually see a notable increase in put volume, even if call volume also rises. This results in a rising put-to-call ratio, a measurement that shows the balance of trading between these contracts. A reading of 1 indicates that put and call volume are equal. A reading above 1 means there are more puts than calls, and a reading below 1 indicates that there are more calls than puts. This information can help analysts understand market sentiment on a stock.

utmost crucial

The Trend Is Your Friend

This is a common phrase among technical analysts. Another saying, which some may find confusing or even annoying, is that "a trend continues until it does not." This means what it says: A trend continues until it is broken. A series of higher highs and higher lows over a period of time comprise a positive trend; a series of lower highs and lower lows comprise a negative trend. One should be able to draw trend lines for both highs and lows that show this clear progression. Sideways trends—also called trendless trends—are built on sideways movements.

Trends can be positive, negative, or sideways; they can also qualify as primary, secondary, or nested. Primary trends are very long-term, built from a decade or more of price history, provided that the investment vehicle has a history that long.

Primary trends govern all other trends nested within them. A stock's primary trend may be positive, for instance, built on a 10-year history of rising prices. A secondary trend, however, might be negative, indicated by a price drop over a year or two. The secondary trend is a counter-trend, also called a corrective trend. For whatever reason, weakness has pushed share price lower—but the primary trend remains intact.

The secondary trend is nestled within the primary trend and may itself contain more nested trends. Even if your main interest is in a currently nested trend, you must pay attention to a stock's primary trend, as the stock is likely to resume following that trend, at least until the trend ends.

Of course, a secondary trend may indicate that one primary trend is ending and a new primary trend is beginning to form. This is especially likely when a bull market primary trend is interrupted by a new bear market trend. A bear market may move faster and with greater volatility than the bull market that preceded it. For example, the 2003–2007 bull market made its gains over four years, as shown in Figure 2.3, the S&P 500 Index (SPX) for the period. Like an explosive charge taking seconds to demolish a structure that took years to build, the subsequent bear market erased four years of gain in just 13 months!

During long trends, investors typically buy and hold investments in a positive trend, or they sell investments short and wait during a negative trend. Investment decisions depend on technical trend analysis, but also on underlying, long-term, fundamental company information. An investor typically expects shares to follow the company's performance expectations for annual earnings, broken down into quarterly reports. Investors anticipate that positions taken this way will be long term. Within those long-term expectations, however, market noise, seasonal factors, corrections, and other factors will create nesting trends that

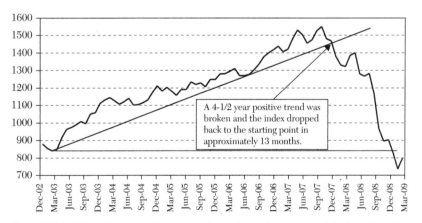

Figure 2.3 S&P 500 Index (SPX) monthly chart shows the trend and the breaking of that trend.

prevent share prices from moving in a single direction for an indefinite time period.

utmost crucial

In general, I like to work within the intermediate-term viewpoint—between three and six months—during long, positive market trends. Doing so lets me build strategies that encompass one and sometimes two quarterly earnings reports, and that take a major portion of the annual seasonal cycle into account. (I may also see many other shorter-term trading opportunities within the charts, which I'll discuss in future chapters.)

A seasonal cycle, which may dominate trading for a period of time, is based on historic positive and negative movements that typically occur during a particular portion of the year.

Volatile or Negative Markets

During volatile markets, which are usually associated with bearish activity, analysts may consider both long-term and intermediate-term trends. History has shown that investors can make profitable trades in these markets, achieving short-term profits and losses as the market makes sharp, quick changes. Many traders take smaller positions in volatile markets than in more stable ones, assigning targets and stop points that result in quick position exits. Such investors are like a baseball team that tries to hit singles and doubles, rather than banking on home runs.

Primary and Secondary Trends

Most investors find that the lion's share of long-term performance comes from bull markets' primary and secondary trends. These trends' consistency and rather cohesive chart patterns keep risk levels relatively low overall. But risk is still present—perhaps at a higher level than usual, as few traders are looking for it. A market that's full of bullish and/or fully invested participants is one that may be running out of the fuel it would need to send it further up. In this situation, investors should be prepared to go on the defensive, looking for trading opportunities while hedging long-term positions when the market corrects itself.

Though primary trends generally govern the ultimate outcomes of all other trends, countertrends or corrections are also opportunities to make money or offset potential losses. Figure 2.4 shows a three-year weekly

Figure 2.4 A weekly Japanese Candlestick chart on Goldman Sachs. Chart courtesy of Bloomberg Professional Service.

candlestick chart. Note the well-formed positive trend channel between lines A and B. Each time the market tested line A, shares encountered resistance and prices reversed—or corrected themselves—within this trend. In fact, the price reversal tested the lower channel line (line B), or at least declined to about halfway between the trend channel lines.

The decline from the trend channel resistance line represents an opportunity. By counting the time period between tops and bottoms, we see that each of these declines lasts between six and 12 weeks before reaching a bottom. In this situation, options may offer better trading opportunities than do selling a position or selling stock short.

The signal is strongest when a short-term or intermediate-term oscillator confirms the top of a trend channel. An oscillator is a technical indicator that uses recent activity to measure shares' momentum and pressure. In Figure 2.5 there is a line under the price chart, labeled RSI. This is the relative strength index, an oscillator that measures overbought and oversold readings based on a stock's movements over 14 periods, typically 14 days. RSI of more than 70 percent typically indicates overbought stock; readings over 80 percent indicate an extremely overbought stock. This confirmation suggests that these shares are

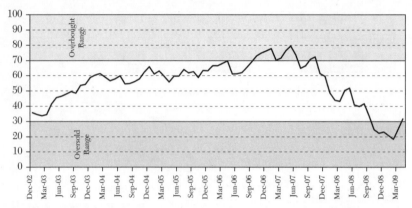

Figure 2.5 A monthly RSI (relative strength index) oscillator on the S&P 500 Index (SPX) monthly chart.

overdue for a correction—but doesn't indicate that a correction will come soon. In fact, the longer that the stock moves higher on overbought readings, the more powerful the positive trend likely is.

utmost critical

As an indicator, RSI typically lags trading momentum. Even so, many analysts wait to see RSI turn lower before confirming a short-term correction within a chart. By doing so, they seek to ensure that they will not miss any short-term upward potential. Of course, they may also wait too long, as shares may ease significantly from their highs after traders test the resistance trend line.

Absolutely critical

Watch the momentum indicator, too. This is a leading indicator, in comparison to RSI, and it may be useful as an alternative to or in conjunction with the RSI. Momentum, which compares the sustained, upward, or downward movement caused by pricing pressure, usually begins to slacken before the underlying stock reverses course, showing that buying pressure may be easing.

First Strategy

This strategy is called covered call overwriting. (It is slightly different from covered call writing, which occurs when a manager buys a stock position and writes a call option against it simultaneously.) The option, to take one example, might be a two- or three-month contract with a strike point that's about 5 percent above the current stock price. If premiums are elevated, a manager may write contracts that are at or just out of the money.

In setting the strike price, evaluate general movement for the stock and the sector—some sectors move more than others—the underlying stock's volatility, momentum, and the potential options contracts' implied volatility. The strike price needn't be 5 percent over the current stock price; that's just an example. In this case, however, it is important to pick a strike price that's higher than the stock price. By doing so, you ensure some upside potential even if the correction does not proceed as expected and shares resume their positive movement.

By writing these call options, you agree to sell your shares at the specified strike price, should the stock rise above that level. In exchange for assuming that obligation, you collect a premium, which can help reduce stock position exposure as the shares enter this corrective phase. The premium may not offset the entire downside exposure but should provide a buffer for the position.

For example, if GS does a full trend channel retracement to the lower trend channel line over a period of eight weeks, we can project a decline of approximately 39 points, or 17 percent. A two-month call with a $240 strike price for 6.20 points can offset 16 percent of the anticipated loss, adding to overall portfolio performance and helping the manager take advantage of the time that the stock is in a corrective phase.

If the share prices rise to or above the strike price, on the other hand, the manager sells the shares for an effective sale price of the strike price of $240 plus the premium collected ($6.20), or $246.20 per share, which is 7.5 percent above the stock's price on the day the options contract sold.

Before the sale, a fund manager may also opt to repurchase the call option, eliminating the risk of a forced stock sale. The repurchase cost may be higher than the original option price. Because option prices and stock prices don't move in perfect concert, however, an option repurchase will possibly end with a net position gain that's larger than the share price gain.

The relationship between the option price and stock price is known as the delta. A delta of 50 percent indicates that the option price will move 50 cents for each dollar that the stock price moves. Deltas change constantly in reaction to stocks' price movements and the relationship between the share price and strike price. As the stock rises above the strike price, the delta will increase. If the stock moves lower, the delta will decline. Deltas range between 0 percent—no correlation between option and stock price—and 100 percent, a perfect correlation between option and stock price.

Put Hedges

In most cases I favor the call overwriting strategy, because it allows managers to take in money rather than spend money. Sometimes, though, calls may not carry sufficient premiums to create a cost-effective strategy. This typically occurs when implied volatility and option premiums are low. In that case, consider purchasing a protective put hedge against the shares.

Put hedges provide protection against a decline in the value of the underlying security by allowing managers to sell those shares at a predetermined strike price, at or before the hedge's expiration date. The effective sale price is the strike price, minus the premium cost for the put. If XYZ's share price is $62.25 and the stock is overbought, for example, you might spend $1.35 per share for a two-month put with a strike price of $60. If shares decline, you have the option of selling the contract, then applying your profit to offset your unrealized loss.

Alternatively, you could exercise the put (wait until expiration, as there is generally no advantage to exercising early) and sell the shares for an effective sale price of $58.65 per share. Should the stock decline shortly after you purchase the put, sell the option for a premium and either buy another put with a lower strike price or sell the stock.

Implied Volatility

Absolutely crucial

Implied volatility, which measures the options risk premium within a contract, generally rises when the underlying instrument declines, and declines when that instrument rises. This is true for both puts and calls. When a stock is overbought, it has typically been on the rise, and therefore implied volatility has likely declined.

A high delta reading is one of the benefits of buying options when implied volatility is low. In-the-money options have intrinsic value, which becomes tied to the relationship between the underlying stock price and the options price. When an option is in the money, its delta should be higher than that of its counterpart. The more a contract is in the money, the more economic value it has. A call and its equivalent put cannot be simultaneously in the money. The lower the volatility, then, the higher the leverage value of a put hedge.

Seasonal Trends

As noted earlier, trends generally sustain themselves over long periods of time. Smaller, shorter-term trends nest within their longer-term counterparts: countertrend movements, known as corrections, and trends that move along with the primary trend. All trends, but especially secondary trends, may be tied to seasonal and/or cyclical factors.

Seasonal trends may be tied to markets, sectors, industry groups, or individual securities. Seasonal trends normally occur annually, but not always—especially during bear markets. The general equities markets typically show a strong, positive seasonal trend that begins at the end of October and ends in the middle of April, with November, December, and January the strongest months of the cycle (and generally the year). Some sectors and groups generally move with that positive trend; others show little or no correlation.

Equities show a generally weak or negative trend during the other portion of the year, between mid-April and late October. September and October are typically the weakest months.

Absolutely crucial!

Cyclical Trends

The overall economy also follows cyclical trends. Growth phases, which follow economic troughs, usually favor growth companies: those with new products and relatively lower overhead. These often attract investors who are looking for new opportunities. Note that growth phases may begin ahead of economic troughs.

Companies that have been around for a while and benefit from sustained trends and sales volume often do best near the peak of an overall economic phase. These companies are often relatively large and well established, and may include those in sectors related to commodities, such as energy and basic materials. (These firms may also benefit from changes in interest rates, economic activity, and currency fluctuations.)

During early cyclical phases, sectors that include technology, communications, and industrial companies often do well. Consumer cyclical stocks usually do well in the middle stages of an upward cycle.

During periods of contraction, associated with slower economic growth and mild recessions, consumer noncyclical, health care, and other defensive groups tend to outperform the broader markets. Figure 2.6 shows an economic cycle and which sectors tend to benefit at different points.

Many sectors are tied to the economic cycle—but stocks, sectors, and the market in general tend to move ahead of the economic cycle, with investors buying stocks before there is clear evidence of an economic upturn. The market is a leading indicator, and many of the yardsticks that measure the economy are lagging indicators. It is very possible to see a measurable upturn or new positive trend develop, even as unemployment reaches a new cycle high or gross domestic product (GDP) sets its cycle low.

Different cycles don't typically move together, or in the same ways. Economic growth cycles usually last longer than contractions. Expansions may last between two and four years, on average, with some extensions to about five years. From 1995 to 2000, the U.S. economy grew at an impressive pace, as the technological revolution fed on Internet access. Recessions tend to last approximately half the length of an expansion, though this is not always the case. The longer a growth cycle lasts, the more damaging the following contraction may be.

One reason that contractions are generally shorter than expansions is that political forces work to stimulate the economy. The Federal Open Market Committee (FOMC) tries to balance the economy between expansion and possible inflation on the one hand, versus contraction and

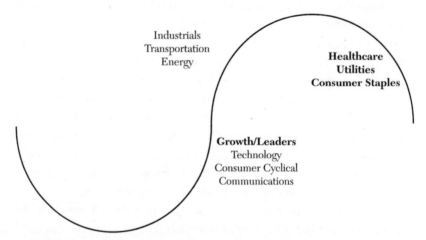

Figure 2.6 Illustration of a typical Economic cycle with sector overlay.

potential deflation on the other, with a primary focus on full employment. During severe economic declines, voters often replace government leaders, especially at the executive level, putting the blame on the incumbent party.

An example appears in the 2008 election of President Barack Obama. The economic decline, which was marked by a sharp and volatile drop in, stock prices, destroyed an enormous amount of wealth. President Bush, Congress, the FOMC, and the Treasury fought a severe and prolonged recession, but voters removed the controlling party in favor of change.

Before taking office, the president-elect and the legislative branch worked toward a record-breaking stimulus program that moved toward building and rebuilding infrastructure, expanding communications access, and getting people and companies back to work. This included a program to keep the automotive industry from going under and an attempt to get the housing market started again after an almost three-year decline. The government also tried to stabilize financial companies and ease credit.

Moves within Moves

In a world of trends within trends, it is very easy to confuse a counter movement with a reversing primary trend. Even market professionals can be slow to label a move as a changed primary trend and may disagree with industry colleagues.

Bear markets, for instance, sometimes contain nested bear market rallies, which can be very strong, very convincing, and actually resemble bull market movements. They may retrace more than one-third, one-half, or even two-thirds of the primary trend decline, showing an impressive gain from the lows.

During these moves, investors should employ conservative strategies to avoid a "bull trap." This occurs when investors buy stocks with the expectation that a new bull market has begun, or that a previous bull cycle has taken control. During conditions with low implied volatility, consider purchasing calls and married/protective puts. During high volatility levels, consider covered combinations and writing puts.

In exchange for accepting the responsibility and risk of potentially buying the representative shares at the strike price, a put seller receives a premium that's based on current conditions.

Covered combinations combine an underlying share purchase with a covered call and put writing strategy. By executing a covered combination, a manager assumes the risk in exchange for collecting a premium on both the call and the put contracts.

Just as there are bull moves within bear markets, there are bear moves within bull markets. These are usually called corrections. Investors—except for bargain hunters—usually show less enthusiasm for corrections than for expansions. Short sales usually accelerate on these movements. The need to cover those short positions can add fuel to the next upward movement, as buy-ins and short squeezes create increased demand. Selling options lets managers benefit from increased volatility and premium levels and may cushion the market's next move.

Nontrends

We have looked at positive and negative trends, but there still is one more trend to consider. Sideways market trends, which some people call nontrends, happen when the market trades in a sustained sideways pattern. The movement may be wide, narrow, or begin as wide and narrow down into a symmetrical triangle or consolidation. This is illustrated in Figure 2.7, which shows a narrowing symmetrical triangle on the weekly chart of Verizon Communications (VZ). Notice that as the pattern progresses lower highs and higher lows are produced.

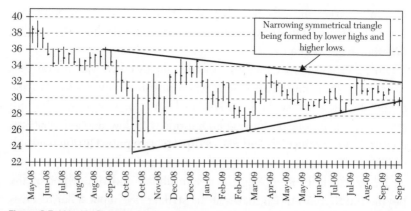

Figure 2.7 Weekly Chart on Verizon Communications.

There are few strategies that work well during sideways trends. Sustained sideways moves have limited potential for gain, and implied volatility levels decline. Option strategies may be workable as a sideways trend begins, but not usable toward the trend's end, especially if that end involves a narrowing or symmetrical triangle trend. Because we.are selling option contracts, the risk of fulfilling option obligations may out-. weigh the potential limited profit.

An investor in this situation might purchase short-term calls on a successful test of the lower trend line/support line and sell those calls on a movement back toward the upper trend line/resistance line, taking lower profits. Or the same investor might buy short-term put contracts upon reaching and testing the upper trend line, then sell those contracts as the lower trend line approaches, again taking small gains. Traders here are a bit like a struggling baseball team, looking for walks and singles.

Understanding the Properties of Trends

In order to understand trends and countertrends, it is important to get a feel for their basic characteristics. This will also help managers create strategies that may be attractive under various conditions.

Analysts look at more than the basic trend pattern. Moving averages are used to verify or invalidate a positive or negative trend. Short-term moving averages are more reactive to trend changes than intermediate-term or long-term moving averages. Confirmation of a positive trend may occur when the shares break above the moving average, and the slope of that moving average turns higher. Conversely, a negative trend may be confirmed when a trend line is broken to the downside and the slope of the trend turns lower. Typical period definitions for short-term moving averages are less than 50 days and less than 10 weeks. Intermediate-term moving averages are between 50 and less than 200 days or 10 weeks to 40 weeks. Long-term averages are more than 200 days or 40 weeks or 10 months. Another measure of confirmation occurs when a shorter period moving average crosses a longer period moving average. For example, if the 50-day moving average crosses over the 200-day moving average, a signal may be generated. Some analysts will also consider the distance between the moving averages. The Moving Average Convergence/Divergence (MACD) indicator, developed by Gerald Apel, compares the

almost crucial

difference of two moving averages for indications of rising or falling momentum between the two averages.

Bull trends tend to last longer than other trends and show rising volume as they continue. Ironically, bull trends often near their ends when most people are bullish, with long position commitments. This can be a good time to hedge those positions.

Positive trends also typically bring contracting option risk premiums. As the perception of risk declines, so do implied volatility levels, in part because upward movements are often smoother than negative trends. Lower premiums may also draw more buyers to purchase options instead of stock, because options are relatively cheap and stock prices much higher than they were when the trend started.

Call volume may also rise for another reason: leverage. Buying call contracts lets investors realize greater percentage gains (and even greater dollar gains), because relative price levels let purchasers buy more calls than stock for the same amount of money. Buyers can also purchase a greater variety of securities with the same capital. We caution against over leveraging.

Analysts often race to upgrade their opinions and target prices during bull markets, particularly those that occur during periods of economic expansion. Even weak stocks may ride the wave.

Bear market rallies also attract buyers, this time to broad-based exchange-traded funds (ETFs). ETFs let buyers minimize their exposure by diversifying. Purchasing contracts allow for performance that's usually lower, but also safer.

Negative trends tend to be sharp, quick, and volatile, with movements that are usually exaggerated compared to the previous bull trend. Volume is usually high on days of extreme downward movement, but may be lower overall than other trends' total volume. Investors often feel an increasing urgency to close positions, minimize exposure, and contain risk as the market declines. This is especially true as benchmarks break critical support levels and psychologically important numbers.

Option premiums may rise sharply as the perception of risk increases. Even during small countertrend rallies, volatility levels may go up and remain elevated. Major bear markets, such as the crash of 1987, the mini-crash of 1989, the downturn following the terrorist attacks of 1993 and 2001, and the market crash of 2008, pushed option premiums to extreme levels. At several points during the 2008 market crash, volatility rose so high that it effectively shut down the options markets and had a significant effect on the equities markets.

Managers who need to be fully invested may reallocate capital investments into defensive sectors and stocks. These share prices usually fall at a slower rate than do growth stock values.

Put option activity generally rises as premiums increase. Writing call options is more attractive due to the increased volatility, but is also more risky. Many fund managers are not allowed to sell naked call options, because of the increased risk of a short-stock squeeze.

When investors and traders jump into put or call option contracts, volume on one will usually rise. (The other may or may not.) When shares decline sharply, put volume usually increases, even if call volume does rise. This creates a rising put-to-call ratio, which shows the trading balance between these contracts. A reading of 1 indicates that put and call volumes are equal. A reading above 1 means more puts than calls; a reading below 1 indicates more calls than puts.

almost critical

At root, trends are fairly simple—but not so simple that nearly anyone can follow them successfully. Other analysis factors, such as continuation and reversal patterns, oscillators, volume, and period-to-period movements, make trends much more complex. In the next chapter we will examine trends further, looking into continuation and reversal patterns.

CHAPTER 3

Trends and Their Ends

CORRECTIONS AND COUNTERTREND MOVEMENTS are part of market action. They provide opportunities to profit from trend reversals, a chance to take profits, and a place to look for new investment opportunities.

Corrective movements are a very healthy part of economic and business cycles, because they often break up prolonged trends. Sustained trends with strong momentum, such as those that form near parabolic movements, can become dangerously overextended very quickly. As history shows, prolonged positive movements—especially those that may be artificially fueled or extended—usually result in the longest, and/or most painful corrections.

A variety of academics and analysts have worked to predict market movements, including Ralph Nelson Elliott, an American accountant and analyst who studied people, economics, markets, and cycles. In his work during the 1930s, he stated that all phenomena have natural waves, and that wave patterns are identifiable and generally repeat themselves. Since these patterns can be identified and tend to repeat themselves, their value for being predictable can be high, especially for those who are able to master them.

Many of these waves confirm and can be used to forecast market movement. According to Elliott, a pattern of five movements produces a wave in a primary trend; three movements typically comprise a corrective wave.

Elliott Waves and Common Trend Analysis

It's not always easy to detect these waves and their changes. What's more, even those who regularly perform Elliott wave analysis must frequently revisit their forecasts for new waves and changes. Even so, it's very interesting to examine the relationship between Elliott wave analysis and common trend analysis. Some analysts use Elliott's ideas to identify nested movements and countertrend actions. Corrections, according to some, fall into this category.

Like other cyclical methods, Elliott wave analysis looks at apparently natural expansion and contraction phases. Wave analysis can be applied to trading vehicles, the economy, business activity, and even political events. Though managers may identify patterns and make projections based on them, these projections are not 100 percent reliable. They often fall short or exceed their goals for both movement and time frame. Cycles tend to vary. If they didn't, forecasting would be foolproof, and model-based computer programs would replace analysts and traders.

Figure 3.1a uses yearly data to show a primary long-term trend for Intel Corp. (INTC). Figure 3.1b shows the same data on a monthly chart; Figure 3.1c offers the same data in a weekly chart. Figure 3.1d shows monthly data, including Elliott wave formations. (Yearly data is difficult to record, as most portfolio managers don't hold positions that long.)

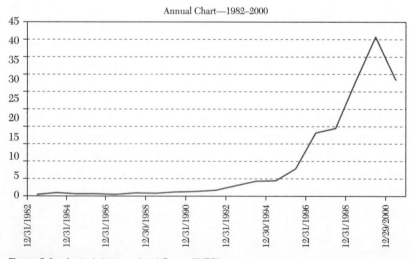

Figure 3.1a Annual chart on Intel Corp. (INTC).

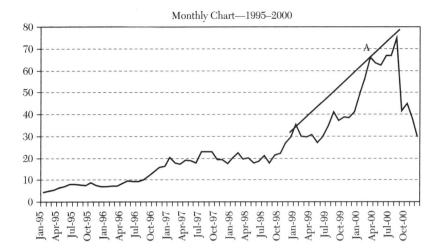

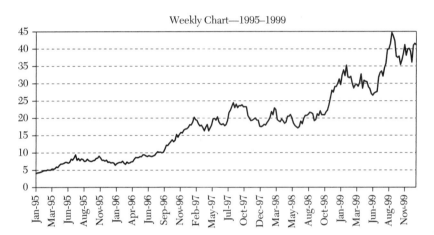

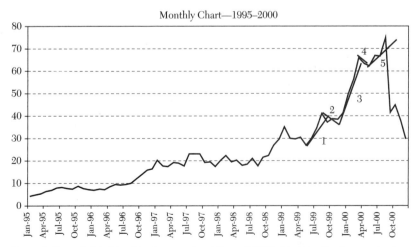

Figure 3.1b, c, d (b) Monthly chart on Intel Corp. (INTC). (c) Weekly chart on Intel Corp. (INTC). (d) Intel Corp. (INTC) monthly chart with Elliott wave illustration.

The charts start and end at the same places, but the roads to those destinations look mighty different. This is largely because the weekly chart shows the nested patterns, countertrend movements, and more market noise than do the annual or even monthly charts.

Investors and traders can use technical analysis and strategies to identify the opportunities and/or risks that these data present. Trends are often more complicated than they first appear, so it's smart to also examine opportunities from countertrends and nested movements.

At point A on the monthly chart, Figure 3.1b, the stock is testing against a long-term trend channel resistance line. In the past, this testing has pushed shares beneath the lower supporting trend channel line. Trend channel lines move in parallel, so we can see that the bottom of the month's trend channel line puts shares 2 points below the resistance line. We can also deduce from earlier patterns, with a high level of probability, that the supporting trend line's test will likely not occur that month, that it will take at least three months to test that point, and the tested price point will be approximately $46, because the line's slope shows an increase of $1.05 per month.

Shareholders could sell their positions and await an opportunity to repurchase them on a test of the supporting trend channel line. But some fund directives require that managers hold or avoid positions for a certain period of time, or stay fully invested in a certain sector or industry group and hold positions if there are no better potential opportunities.

Such managers may find this an opportunity to write calls against the long stock position. As we saw in the last chapter, this is a method of potentially enhancing returns by collecting premiums and profiting from a countertrend movement.

Investors could also potentially profit from purchasing a put contract or a bear put spread. Because we believe it will take three months, in this instance, for the corrective movement to arrive, we can choose a strategy that generally matches that time expectation. We can usually find options contracts with one and two months until expiration; the next contract will expire in three to five months, depending on the expiration cycle of that security's options contracts.

Many funds are "long only," allowed to purchase only stock and maintain only positive positions. Some of these funds don't permit offsetting hedges. Market activity, such as the downturns of 2001–2002, the crash of

1987, or the meltdown of 2008, have sometimes pushed funds to change their directives, adding the ability to use option strategies to hedge positions or to take offsetting positions in an effort to control risk. Many funds are examining their charters and mandates, seeking to change them in order to trade or, at the least, be able to hedge positions in the future.

A stock's movements back to the supporting trend line may not completely meet expectations. The stock may stop short of the trend line, violate the trend line, or even produce a trend reversal. Monitor the movement and take appropriate action as necessary.

Nesting Patterns

Managers can find yet more information in the weekly and daily charts. The daily chart may provide too much information, but may also contain early indications of weekly chart patterns. (In general, five days of daily chart data produces data for one weekly chart period. Four to five weeks of weekly data comprise a monthly chart; between 20 and 23 days of daily data can also form a monthly chart.)

Figure 3.2 is a combined chart that shows how a weekly chart may nest within a monthly chart. Note the negative reversal that begins

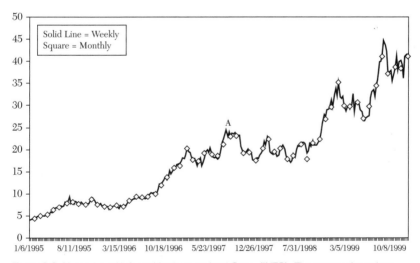

Figure 3.2 Nested weekly/monthly chart on Intel Corp. (INTC). The square dot points represent the monthly closing prices and the line represents the weekly closing pricings.

at point A, breaking the weekly formation's positive trend but staying within the boundaries of the monthly chart's positive formation. This is an ideal way to see nesting patterns and trends. The longer primary trend dominates until it fails. Managers can improve performance by investing for the primary trend and trading around it within intermediate-term and short-term movements, such as the ones shown by the nested weekly chart.

Nested chart patterns may occur within an ongoing primary pattern, but may also produce early signs that their parent patterns are near failure. The nested pattern may break its parent's supporting trend channel line, an indication that the parent trend is now in trouble. This early warning may come during the first week of a month, thereby giving three to four weeks of notice before month's end. Recognizing these relationships and their relevance is important. Failure to see these con-nections may mean lost capital and unrealized profits.

In most cases, failing trends show early warning signs. Those same early warning signs, however, may also point to a pause during which a trend takes a break, often to relieve overbought or oversold conditions. A pause may even be a correction, as some managers take profits or reduce risk exposure.

Continuation Patterns

Charted pauses are known as "continuation patterns." A continuation pattern is usually a temporary halt in the prevailing trend. This is typically a time to take a break, build up energy, collect new resources, and evalu-ate the reasons behind past movements. A positive trend that moved too fast, for instance, might encounter significant selling pressure that knocks buyers down the chart.

Continuation patterns usually change a trend's direction from up or down to sideways; the direction often depends on the trend bias, as well as on the price support or resistance it encounters. In this case, support means that sellers encounter resistance from buyers who won't tolerate prices falling below a certain level. Resistance happens when buyers cannot move shares above a certain price, because of the large numbers of sellers at that level. At these points, bulls and bears converge.

Continuation patterns occur in both positive and negative charts, often coming about after a security reaches extended movements, has overbought or oversold oscillator readings, or has generally moved in one direction for a particular length of time.

Continuation or Reversal?

There are times, however, when a continuation pattern looks like or even becomes a reversal pattern. Some continuation and reversal patterns may look alike, making it more difficult for a portfolio manager to arrive at a clear-cut interpretation. A movement may begin as a continuation trend, for instance, then change to a reversal pattern as the market incorporates new information.

Most technical analysts use stops or hedges to protect against unanticipated reversals and to give a manager room to monitor a position. Unexpected events, such as a surprisingly strong earnings announcement or a factory catastrophe, can send the stock price down and also change chart patterns. That's particularly true in the short and intermediate terms, where movements can be volatile and extreme, but news can also affect a long-term outlook.

Figure 3.3a shows a bowl-like formation that could be a negative consolidation pattern, one that lets selling pressure ease off an oversold

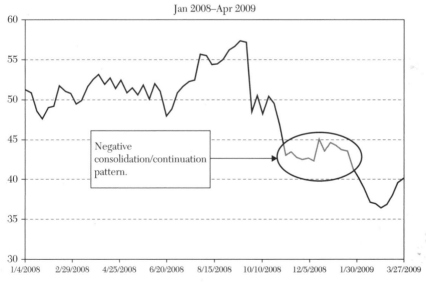

Figure 3.3a Kellogg Co. (K) weekly chart illustrating a rounding bottom formation.

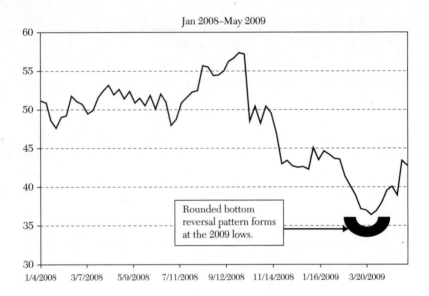

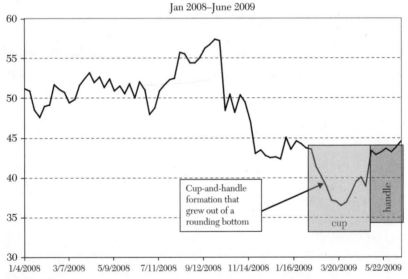

Figure 3.3b, c (b) Kellogg Co. (K) weekly chart illustrating a rounding bottom/upward reversal formation with progression. (c) Kellogg Co. (K) weekly chart illustrating a cup-and-handle formation that was an outgrowth of a rounding bottom.

stock (and at the same time attracts more sellers). Figure 3.3b shows a slight upturn in performance. Have the bears exhausted their ability to push shares lower? Have the bulls mustered enough strength to overwhelm the bears?

Figure 3.3c shows sideways movement: perhaps a negative continuation pattern, but also possibly a positive reversal pattern known as a "cup-and-handle" formation. Cup-and-handles are common positive reversal patterns, but there's no certainty until a positive, sustained upward move confirms a positive reversal.

Bears who are short the stock may wish to purchase protective calls against their short positions or place a stop between 2 and 4 percent above the handle low. Another option may involve buying the position back, then either writing calls against it or purchasing puts to maintain a negative position. Regardless of which strategy you choose, closely watch the $44.11 level, which is 3 percent above the handle low price of $42.83. A break above that level may be an indication of a new positive trend movement, which would have a negative impact on bearish positions. Managers should carefully monitor, close, or modify positions based on the fund's risk/reward profile and expectations.

Those who didn't take action during the rounding bottom pattern should definitely move when the sideways handle begins to form. A rounding bottom, also known as a "fry-pan" bottom, confirms a positive reversal pattern with a break above the left side of the resistance formed just above the pattern's bowl portion. A break above that resistance means that a positive reversal is very likely, so those with short or negative positions should move to protect their investments.

Bullish investors can also benefit from positive reversal patterns, like the fry-pan bottom and cup-and-handle formation, because these patterns help buyers acquire shares near their lows.

Other strategies are also possible. Two of my favorites, covered combinations and writing naked puts, help bullish managers take advantage of a reversal and the rise in implied volatility levels that accompanies share price declines. Purchasing a bull spread is yet another option.

The pattern also helps managers create a mental stop point, using consolidation supports, to protect against further downward movement.

Opposing Reversal Patterns

Each reversal pattern has an opposing reversal pattern. A positive reversal pattern, such as a fry-pan bottom, has a topping pattern, which in this case is a rounding top, shown in Figure 3.4. Invert the reversal or its opposite, and the two charts look nearly the same.

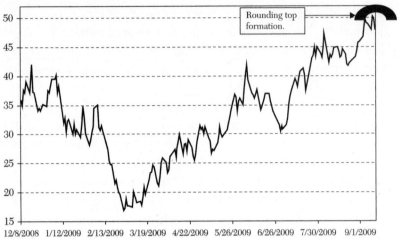

Figure 3.4 U.S. Steel Corp. (X) daily chart showing rounding top formation.

Many analysts consider head-and-shoulders patterns the most popular reversal patterns. They're generally reliable and usually easy to identify. When they do fail, that failure is easy to see—and a meaningful signal in itself.

Head-and-shoulders patterns appear at both the tops and the bottoms of charts. The head-and-shoulders top pattern in Figure 3.5a looks just like a person from the back. I have labeled the left shoulder "LS," the head as "H," the right shoulder as "RS," the neckline as "NL," and a shoulder line as "SL." The neckline break completes the pattern.

Calculate an initial price objective by determining the distance from the neckline to the head at the head's horizontal point, then subtracting that number from the neckline at its breaking point. The top of the head, set the second week of October, was $41.99. The neckline at that point was approximately $38.70. The difference of $3.29 ($41.99 – $38.70) could be projected as a downside target once the neckline is broken, completing the pattern.

Head-and-shoulders reversal patterns are often symmetrical, with the left and right shoulders forming over roughly equivalent lengths of time. This symmetry allows analysts and managers to anticipate the point at which to initiate or close a position, thereby lowering risk.

Figure 3.5b is a head-and-shoulders bottom formation. Note that the pattern looks nearly identical to the head-and-shoulders top, except

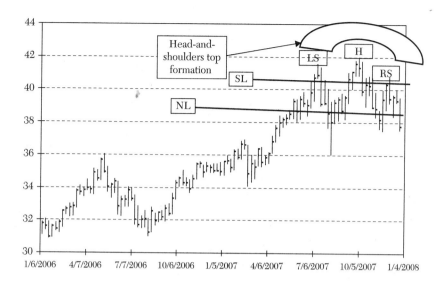

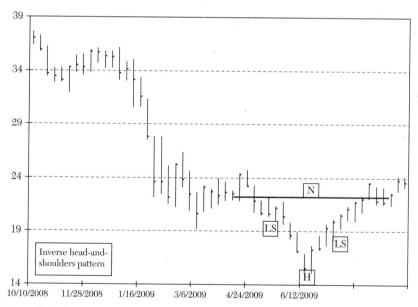

Figure 3.5a, b (a) Select Sector SPiDR Industrial (XLI) weekly chart showing a head-and-shoulders top formation. (b) Select Sector SPiDR Industrial (XLI) weekly chart showing an inverse head-and-shoulders pattern.

that it is inverted. Once again I have labeled the parts of the pattern and have counted the periods on the left shoulder and projected them out on the right shoulder. This provides a timing opportunity by helping us anticipate when the pattern will be complete. Like the head-and-shoulders top pattern mentioned earlier, we can obtain our first target by calculating the difference from the bottom (extreme) of the head to the neckline on that date, then adding that value to the neckline when it breaks out.

These head-and-shoulders patterns are simple and easy to see. Other head-and-shoulders patterns are more complex and might be skewed (this is common), have more than one clear head, or incorporate parts of other patterns. More complicated head-and-shoulders patterns still offer functional reversals and valid signals, but they can be difficult to spot and may lack the symmetry of less complex patterns.

Relatively small head-and-shoulders patterns, with the head slightly above (top pattern) or below (bottom pattern) the shoulder line, may not appear as a head-and-shoulders reversal pattern. This takes some training to spot.

Complex patterns also require more careful analysis. Horizontally compressed patterns or those with lots of noise may be hard to read. Other factors, such as numerous indicators, moving averages, and technical tools, may also complicate a chart. Try zooming in on the chart, focusing on just the area in question plus a slight overlap outside that pattern.

In many cases, a reversal pattern also materializes a second time, this time as an inverse of the first reversal pattern. This is another form of symmetry. The market, it seems, likes balance. As investors and traders we can benefit from that knowledge by keeping a watchful eye toward the formation of such patterns, which may result in a more favorable price action. It is important to keep an objective eye as well, as other patterns may form before the one you are anticipating. Strategies, ranging from aggressive to conservative, may help managers navigate both positive and negative reversals.

CHAPTER 4

Building Strategies around Reversal and Continuation Patterns

SO FAR WE'VE EXPLORED TRENDS, as well as reversal and continuation patterns. Reversal patterns usually reverse or halt the prevailing trend; continuation patterns offer a sort of "rest period" for a prevailing trend. In this chapter we'll discuss prevalent reversal and continuation patterns, outline strategies that can be used in conjunction with them, and look at instances where these patterns may fail.

Spotting Reversal and Continuation Patterns

Many technical analysts are justifiably proud of their ability to discern reversal and continuation patterns. But the charts can play tricks on even the best analyst, offering false patterns, patterns that turn into other patterns, complex patterns, and pattern failures. I pay special attention to patterns' subtle characteristics, using a variety of techniques to help identify and monitor patterns.

Confirming Patterns Using Different Time Frames

As we noted in Chapter 3, reversal and continuation patterns can occur in longer- and shorter-term patterns or within nested trends.

Patterns can also emerge as analysts switch time frames, very often when going from a shorter-term chart to a longer-term chart. There are many instances in which an analyst may find one pattern in a daily chart, for instance, and another pattern in a weekly chart. The patterns may be very similar, with the longer-term chart offering a more condensed version but a more condensed pattern, since it covers the same time span, say two months, but the view between a two-month daily and two-month weekly chart is compressed in time, using fewer points to mark the activity. Different charts provide different views of the data: a condensed version with less intramonth noise, and a second version with more data in greater detail. It's a bit like switching a camera lens from wide view to telephoto. The items in the viewfinder don't change—but how you see them does.

utmost crucial

Figure 4.1a is a daily chart on Mastercard Inc. (MA). This graph shows a head-and-shoulders top pattern, with labels identifying the left shoulder (LS), head (H), right shoulder (RS), neckline (NL), shoulder line (SL), and first price target (T). Note the chart trend lines and numbers on the left and right shoulders, which mark the number of periods. This helps us anticipate some future movements based on the rule of symmetry, which states that the right shoulder should be about the same length as the left shoulder. (It's not uncommon for one shoulder to be a few periods longer or shorter than the other.)

utmost crucial

Figure 4.1b is the same chart as Figure 4.1a, with the addition of the relative strength index (RSI) oscillator, the momentum indicator, which we'll examine in greater detail in later chapters, and corresponding pattern identification marks. Comparing these two charts offers a good way to confirm an emerging pattern.

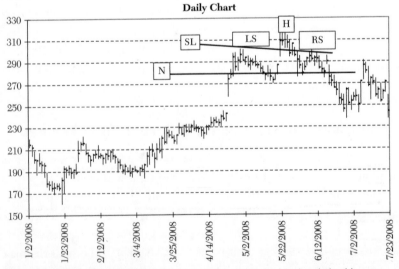

Figure 4.1a Daily chart on Mastercard Inc. (MA) showing a head-and-shoulders top pattern, with shoulder and neck lines.

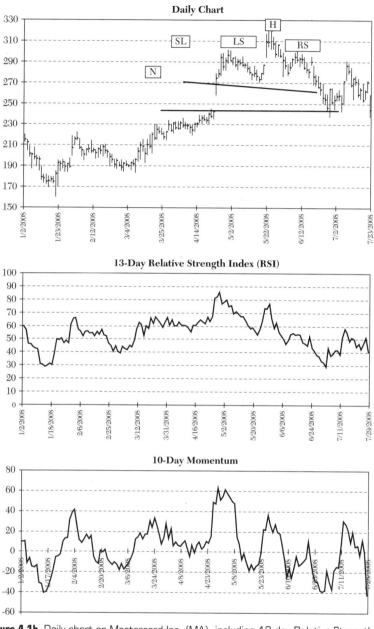

Figure 4.1b Daily chart on Mastercard Inc. (MA), including 13-day Relative Strength Index (RSI) and 10-day momentum gauge.

Note the volume histogram at the foot of each chart. Volume is crucial to any chart, helping measure buying and selling pressure, illustrating where significant buyers or sellers may be waiting, and indicating whether a

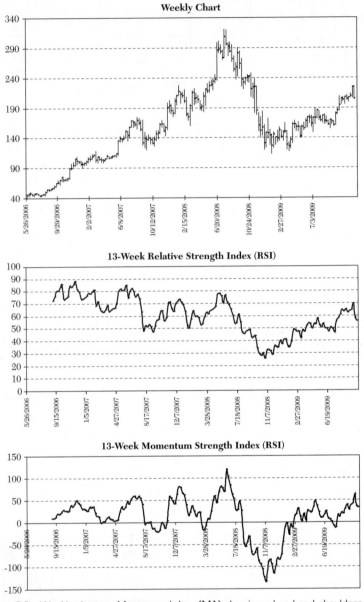

Figure 4.1c Weekly chart on Mastercard Inc. (MA) showing a head-and-shoulders top pattern with support and resistance lines and first target.

trend is gaining or losing steam. The volume histogram often has a similar pattern to that of the price chart.

In Figures 4.1a and 4.1b volume has risen and peaked, coinciding with the head of the head-and-shoulder pattern. This indicates that sellers at the $28.00 level met with willing buyers, preventing the price from advancing.

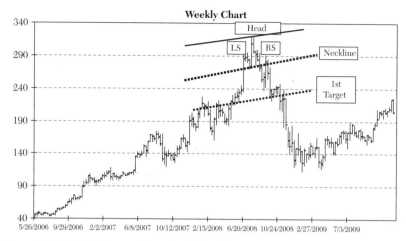

Figure 4.1d Weekly chart on Mastercard Inc. (MA) with 13-week Relative Strength Index (RSI) and 13-week momentum gauge. (e) Weekly chart on Mastercard Inc. (MA) with neckline break and target illustration.

Figure 4.1d shows the same data, this time computed weekly. It shows the head-and-shoulders pattern over the same time frame (identified here with markings that correspond to those in Figure 4.1a.) I've also framed the daily time period, isolating this section from the rest of the time period.

Compare these two graphs, and you'll see that they produce similar patterns, albeit over a month or more. This confirms an intermediate-term reversal, which may indicate an intermediate-term correction: one in which the long-term, positive, primary trend continues, but the nested, intermediate-term pattern is about to turn negative.

Of course, this could also be the first indication that the primary trend is changing, or that the longer-term trend is entering a continuation phase. It's not always easy to know which, in part because the correction that forms from a reversal pattern may often stretch to more than two—or even three—times the length of the head-to-neckline measurement. Longer-term patterns, such as those shown on the monthly chart, may also begin to break down in the presence of a correction, forming a reversal pattern on the primary trend. This is especially likely toward the end of economic expansion, or when the ascending portion of a business cycle is nearing its peak.

Building Pattern-Based Strategies

Figure 4.1d is another look at Figure 4.1a, this time showing the neckline break and the chart's move to the first measured target point: the point to which we expect the stock price will fall, though stock values often eventually exceed this target. Calculate the first measured target in a head-and-shoulders pattern by subtracting the distance between the top of the head ($309) and the neckline on that date ($280.37), then subtracting that difference from the neckline on the day that the neckline breaks (point A).

In this case, the first measured target is $251.74—information that's helpful in setting up a strategy. Speculators might purchase a long put or bear put spread, reasoning that they'll achieve maximum profit at the target point. A long put strategy simply means buying a put with unlimited profit potential (down to zero on the underlying stock price) and a maximum risk that's equal to the premium paid. A bear spread involves purchasing an at-the-money contract and selling an out-of-the-money contract (one with a lower strike price than the purchased contract). Limited, maximum profit occurs at the lower strike price; maximum risk occurs at the upper strike price, which is also the spread's total cost. Managers might hedge to that level, or may be willing to risk movement. This is especially true for long-only funds, which may be prohibited from taking offsetting positions. If the distance is not too great, the manager may elect to place a stop and exit the long position on a violation of that measured target. The stop order sits just below the target and becomes a sell order after touching the stop point.

Some funds are only allowed to write covered calls, also called covered overwriting strategies. Managers of such funds might sell a call one or two months before expiration, with a strike price between the neckline and head. It's unlikely that share prices will reverse, rise, and ultimately be called away, unless the market cycle is in a strong bullish phase or news events affect share prices.

In that case, a correction will likely leave the longer-term pattern virtually unaffected and simultaneously provide buying opportunities for new and existing purchasers. Many professionals believe that this scenario can offer low risks and high rewards, especially because it often occurs when fundamental company results—earnings and business expansion decisions—are already evident.

If it's within a fund's mandate, purchasing short-term puts may be an even more economically attractive strategy, especially when the bull market phase is intact. Positive trends usually lead to lower implied volatility levels, so protection using puts may be more attractive than writing calls, particularly toward the end of a calendar year.

Put price appreciation can help offset a position's decline in value. Many managers are evaluated on their performance over set time periods, so an offsetting hedge can limit a decline's impact on fund performance without requiring that a manager sell, then repurchase a stock position. (Many funds require that managers wait—sometimes as much as a year—before repurchasing stock. By relying on repurchase, such a fund could easily miss a stock's most significant move.)

When volatility levels are slightly elevated, a fund manager may compensate for higher option premiums by selling an out-of-the-money put and buying an in-the-money put. This may limit the downside risk, help control the hedge cost, and mitigate a potential loss from the long put, should the stock achieve its downside goals and reverse higher during the period before option expiration. The spread position will also help control the break-even price level for the underlying security, based on the long put purchase price.

More Complex Patterns: The Double Top

The head-and-shoulders pattern in Figures 4.1a through d is relatively easy to identify—but not all patterns are so simple.

Figure 4.2 shows a complex head-and-shoulders top pattern. This pattern is similar to a conjoined twin, with two heads and three shoulders.

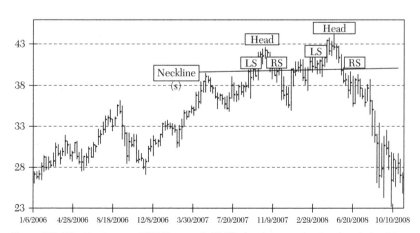

Figure 4.2 Weekly chart on CVS Caremark (CVS) showing complex head-and-shoulders top pattern.

Many analysts call this a double top. Note the two peaks with nearly identical price levels. Bears are holding this price, refusing to let the bulls move the stock above it. Ultimately a reversal will push the bulls lower, or they will gain enough energy to break above that resistance level. A retreat and another upward movement may produce a triple top.

Each failure to break through a particular price point raises the importance of that resistance point. Should the bulls ultimately overcome resistance, the significance of that break will depend on the number of previous failed attempts to push higher. Furthermore, short covering and new demand may create the fuel to push the shares higher.

As a stock price stalls, bullish investors may lose confidence and exit their long positions. Managers may decide that the upward movement is unlikely to reach their upside target, or that the position is taking too much time and capital. In this situation, consider selling the stock and reinvesting a smaller amount of capital into longer-term call options. This lets the manager use the bulk of the capital for other investments and still maintain a long position in the shares.

A manager might also write short-term out-of-the-money calls against the long call, creating a calendar (or diagonal spread) that's meant to lower the position's overall cost. On the downside, however, this strategy can lead to sacrificed opportunity if the stock suddenly heads up.

Figure 4.3a flips our view, showing an inverse head-and-shoulders reversal pattern. The pattern is skewed, making it more difficult to identify. Figure 4.3b is the same graph, this time with labels attached, to help

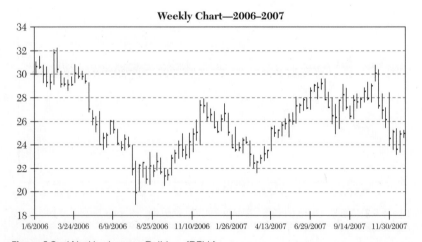

Figure 4.3a Weekly chart on Dell Inc. (DELL).

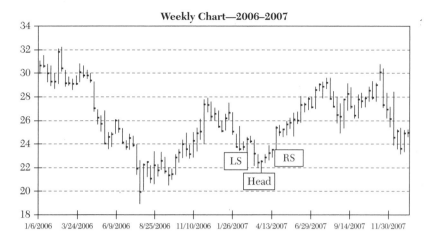

Figure 4.3b, c (b) Weekly chart on Dell Inc. (DELL) showing inverse head-and-shoulders pattern with labels. (c) Daily chart on Manpower Inc. (MAN) showing positive reversal/double bottom, accompanied by momentum and oscillator reversals. Additionally, note the volume breakout several weeks later as the stock breaks above resistance.

with pattern recognition. The pattern still has a head and two shoulders—though you may need to turn the chart on its side to see them.

Like negative reversal patterns, positive reversal patterns also have characteristics that may be seen in their oscillators, momentum, and volume patterns. Figure 4.3c shows these identifying patterns. Positive reversal patterns are generally subtler, because there is usually less interest in negative trends than in positive ones. Volume is usually muted, compared to positive charts, and changes in the oscillators and technical gauges tend to lag.

In this chart, we measure the first objective in a way that's similar to the process we used for the head-and-shoulders top. Take the difference from the bottom of the head and the neckline on that date the head formed, then add it to the neckline on the date of the positive breakout. Or use the symmetry property. Once again, the number of periods between the left shoulder and the head should be equivalent to the number between the head and the right shoulder.

Figure 4.4 shows a complex inverse head-and-shoulders pattern, also known as a double-bottom or a "W" pattern, produced only when the stock declines sharply into its first low. (More gradual descents or a more neutral pattern may not produce the "W.") Triple and even quadruple bottoms may also form.

The more times a bottom holds against testing, the more significant its support at that level. A break shows that bears mustered enough strength to overpower bulls who had held that level, so the bearish trend will likely continue—and perhaps accelerate. Volatility levels will likely rise; they typically move higher as stock prices fall.

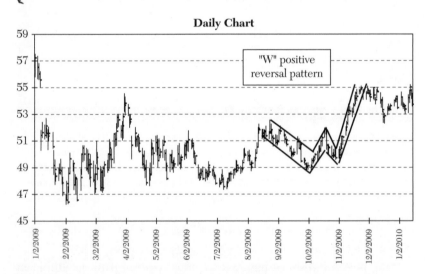

Figure 4.4 Wal-Mart Stores (WMT) daily chart illustrating the positive "W" reversal pattern.

Managers might sell their positions and look for better places to put any remaining capital, especially if they have notable unrealized losses in the stock.

Those that hold the shares should consider a hedge for their positions. A bearish three-way strategy is potentially a good choice, given the situation's high implied volatility. Buy a bear spread using puts: an at-the-money long put and an out-of-the-money short put. Consider writing (selling) an out-of-the-money call option to help finance the purchase. This strategy limits upside potential, but makes purchasing the bear spread more feasible.

Alternatively, a manager might sell both the stock shares and an out-of-the-money put option. The manager could then repurchase the shares, should they decline below the put's strike price, at an effective cost of the strike price, less the premium received.

For an example, consider a scenario in which our graphed stock tested the $50.80 level twice, and a fund manager feared that support would be broken. He sold the shares at face value, then sold a two-month put with a strike price of $47.50 for $2.15. If the stock erodes further and breaks the put strike price before its expiration, he could repurchase the stock for an effective price of $45.35 (strike minus put premium), if the put is assigned. This ultimately creates alpha by not only containing a loss but through recapturing the position at a new, lower cost basis.

For a slightly longer view, look at Figure 4.5, a weekly chart for the data that Figure 4.4 covers daily. A positive reversal pattern is clearly forming,

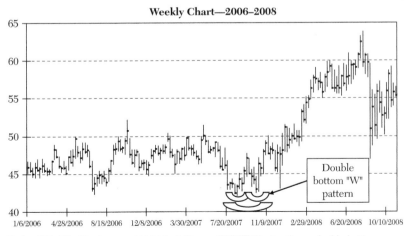

Figure 4.5 Weekly chart on Wal-Mart Stores (WMT) illustrating a double bottom or "W" formation.

but without the detail that the daily chart offers. Some may say this is a noise reduction; others may say that the analysis has lost valuable data.

A longer view may indicate that the reversal pattern is nested within a primary or longer-term trend. A break at the double bottom, or "W," may be a first indication that the longer-term chart pattern may be in jeopardy, making the new pattern all the more important.

Continuation Patterns

We have looked at charts in two general categories: trends and reversals. Now it is time to look at the third category: continuation patterns.

As the name suggests, a continuation pattern occurs when an interrupted trend is expected to resume. It is a pause in the larger pattern. In many cases a continuation involves a band of sideways trading, which may or may not break a supporting trend channel line.

Most continuation patterns fall into two general patterns: flags and pennants. A flag has a square or rectangular form; pennants tend to be more triangular. Other formations take the shape of back-to-back triangles, or diamond patterns and expanding wedges. All of these share some characteristics, mainly the ability to bring a trend to a temporary halt.

Figure 4.6 shows a flag at half mast pattern. Note how the shares of this stock ran up to the $9.34 level and then fell back, only to move in a sideways pattern. Throughout the pattern, the distance from the resistance trend line (labeled R) is nearly equal to that from the support

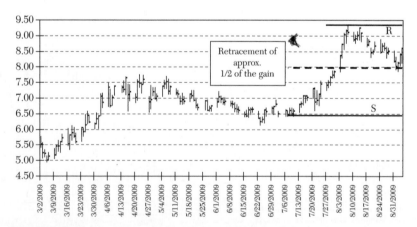

Figure 4.6 Southwest Airlines (LUV) daily chart showing a flag at half mast pattern.

trend line (labeled S). There is little evidence that the pattern is narrowing between the mast of the flagpole and the open end of the flag.

Figure 4.7a shows a descending triangular formation. The resistance trend line (labeled R) declines from the start toward an intersection with the supporting trend line (labeled S). The intersection of these lines is known as the apex. The form is more of a pennant, just like a ball game pennant. Most pennant formations resolve within about two-thirds of the distance between their beginning and the apex. Trend lines converge at the apex.

In this descending triangle, we see that the bears gain some strength as the pattern progresses, limiting bullish moves. This is actually a strategy play in which the bulls firmly hold their scrimmage point: the supporting trend line. Bears may attempt to push below that, holding the bulls back from a recovery. Bulls ultimately push above the bears' offensive line with a positive breakout above the resistance trend line. Figure 4.7b shows this pattern, breaking higher.

Managers can turn this situation into an opportunity. In cases where volatility has abated, a portfolio could sell some out-of-the-money puts as an alternative to increasing share positions.

This has several advantages. The fund takes on no additional positions—at least initially—so it commits only the capital needed for the short put margin. A positive breakout should mean declining put value. That would let the manager either cover that position for a gain, or allow the put to expire worthless, capturing the entire premium. A manager

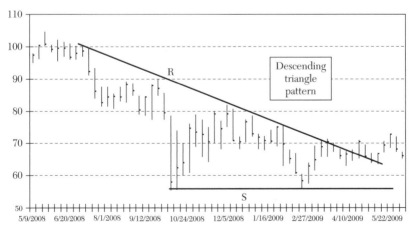

Figure 4.7a Weekly chart on Chevron Corp. (CVX) showing descending triangle.

Figure 4.7b Weekly chart on JB Hunt (JBHT) showing ascending triangle.

could also realize the gain by repurchasing the puts, which would also free up the naked option's margin requirement. Depreciation of premium over time works for the put writer in this case, allowing for some profit even if the stock does not appreciate.

A manager might also take advantage of the situation by selling a portion of the position, as well as some out-of-the-money calls and out-of-the-money puts. The goal is to take some profit now, sell part of the remaining position at prices that might be between 5 percent and 10 percent higher, and consider repurchasing the sold-off portion of the position when it reaches a price that's between 5 percent and 10 percent below current market value.

This strategy takes advantage of a combination of time decay, depreciation, volatility, economic depreciation, and active management in a market that many may consider stagnant. A manager might also measure one-third of the distance from the pattern's apex and use option contracts that expire around that time. Remember, though, that this strategy limits the upside movement for the remaining shares and may mean that the fund repurchases sold shares during an unexpected reversal.

The ascending triangle is the opposite of the descending triangle. This pattern is usually a continuation pattern when the trend interrupted is bearish. Bulls advance toward the bear line, which the bears fight to hold. As the pattern progresses, so does bullish movement, but without a break through bearish lines.

An Amazon.Com Example

In February 2009 Amazon.com (AMZN) shares entered a period of consolidation, following a positive reversal pattern. This continued into the fourth-quarter earnings report, when the company reported that earnings rose to $0.52 per share, beating consensus estimates of $0.50 per share. The positive earnings report was a surprise, given the weak economy and its impact on the retail sector. Good earnings news and positive company comments led to investor buying.

In Figure 4.8a we see that the stock gapped higher, jumping above the 21-day moving average and the upper Bollinger Band line. A volume spike accompanied the breakout. Many investors obeyed this signal to either take or add to a position in Amazon.com stock. The stock continued to rise on the day following the breakout, pushing the oscillators further into overbought territory. Note how the money flow indicator (MF) on the chart rose to a new five-month high.

Figure 4.8b is a weekly chart on AMZN. The chart shows a positive irregular head-and-shoulders reversal pattern with a short consolidation that extended off the right shoulder (RS).

This was a tricky chart, as it nearly produced a failure of the inverse head-and-shoulder pattern. Prior to the reversal's breakout, a would-be buyer might have been enticed to write out-of-the-money puts. Implied volatility was at 77.63 percent, resulting in a premium of $1.60 for a 49-day put contract with a $40 strike price. (We used a strike price just under the $42.70 support, shown on the chart.)

After the breakout, the put's value dropped to $0.55. The price hike—and the stock movement behind it—not only benefited the put contract, but also lessened the implied volatility level, which dropped when risk perception declined. Traders and short-term investors could have repurchased that contract for a profit of $1.05.

Managers could have used several strategies at or near the breakout. Just before the breakout, when things appeared a bit uncertain, a fund might have bought a half position in the underlying security and written a three-month call with a $60 strike and a three-month put with a $35 strike, creating a covered combination. This could be done for a net debit of $41.20 per share.

In this strategy, the hope is that the stock will rise to the $60 strike, producing a profit of $18.47 per share, or 77.6 percent. If share prices

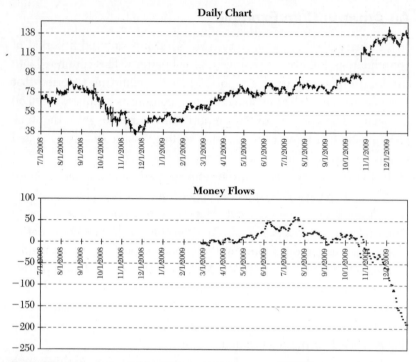

Figure 4.8a Daily chart and Money Flows on Amazon.com (AMZN).

Figure 4.8b Weekly chart on Amazon.com (AMZN) showing complex inverse head-and-shoulders pattern.

stayed unchanged until the options' expiration, a fund would net a profit of $8.47 per share, or 35.6 percent. The risk, however, is that the stock could decline below the $35 strike price. The fund would then purchase the remaining half position for an effective average cost basis of $38.26 per share for the whole position.

Trends create the greatest money-making opportunities, because they usually continue for a workable period of time. In reversals, managers get caught when the prevailing trend ends. Continuation patterns provide opportunities for both profit and loss, because many traders become confused. Creating strategies for these patterns can help investors successfully manage portfolios and navigate continuation and reversal patterns.

CHAPTER 5

Oscillators

DURING OUR TRAVELS THUS FAR through the study of technical analysis, we have discussed oscillators in passing. Many technicians rely on oscillators to confirm buy or sell signals; others rely on oscillators as a primary signal for opportunities to enter or exit positions. Whichever method you choose, oscillators can make the difference between profit and loss, opportunity and misfortune.

The term *oscillator* implies that prices oscillate between ranges or extremes, sometimes straying from a range but eventually normalizing. Oscillators don't forecast a trend or indicate a new trend's beginning. Instead, they measure movement within a trend, tracking an underlying instrument's movements with respect to time and price changes.

utmost crucial

Oscillators can offer signals that last days, weeks, or months, helping analysts make better use of charts that cover varying time frames. Considering trends and oscillators in tandem can provide a greater advantage than just looking at trends, because oscillator signals can help time a strategy or investment.

Though they are always legitimate tools, oscillators don't always work. No indicator does. When you use oscillators, it's important to consider their performance in light of the overall trend. An oscillator that appears to fail, for instance, may itself be a signal, showing that the instrument's prevailing movement is so strong that an oscillator reading of "overbought" or "oversold" may continue for a while.

Absolutely critical

There are probably more than 30 published oscillators and a countless number of proprietary, nonpublished oscillators. We will look at

63

some of the most popular oscillators, understand what they are and how they work, and discuss the importance of matching the oscillator you intend to use with the movement of the product you'll track. Some oscillators work better than others in specific market conditions. I typically use several oscillators and other technical indicators to gain both insight and confirmation.

Oscillator Types

One of the most popular oscillators is the relative strength index (RSI). Invented by J. Welles Wilder, the famed developer of many technical tools, RSI measures two dynamics at once: time and the force of price movements. Stronger moves lead to stronger, extended readings. Wilder found that, by comparing an instrument's movement over 14 periods (to itself), an analyst can determine the strength of that movement and time it to understand if it has peaked or troughed, or if it is extended or overextended.

Many analysts use RSI through daily charts over either a 13- or 14-day period. A weekly chart might use an 8- or 13-week period; monthly observations may use a 5-, 8-, or 13-month period. Recently, periods of 9 days (or occasionally weeks) have become popular.

Analysts tend to gravitate toward certain period lengths for different reasons. One is that certain periods fit the calendar. A 21-day period represents a month's worth of trading. Other periods, such as 13 days, are numbers within the Fibonacci sequence, or within other natural number sequences that some analysts believe are strongly relevant to trading patterns and cycles.

RSI uses a scale of 0 to 100. An RSI reading of more than 70 generally indicates overbought conditions; a reading below 30 generally indicates that an instrument may be oversold. Positive signals can occur on movements from below 30 to above 30; negative signals can occur on movements that cross below 70 from an overbought reading.

Figure 5.1 shows the movement of Staples Inc. (SPLS). Within the overall negative trend, RSI may peak below 70, rather than following the general rule that levels around 70 show an overbought condition.

In this case, however, the negative trend skews the indicator. In light of the negative trend, we can use a lower RSI reading as an overbought

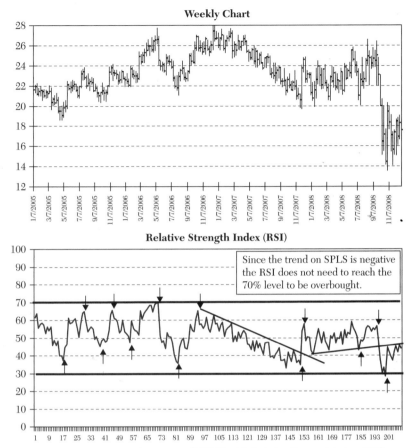

Figure 5.1 Weekly chart on Staples Inc. (SPLS) with Relative Strength Index (RSI).

signal. We can also draw trend lines along the peaks and troughs of this ~~indicator~~ to illustrate when the shares are approaching overbought or oversold readings. *cruc nl*

We may also adjust the oversold reading. The chart shows that the stock did not become oversold until RSI dropped toward 20, not the standard 30. This is very common, especially for stocks or other vehicles with strong negative trends.

Just as we adjust the oversold signal point, we can also adjust the overbought reading. We might see overbought readings rise from 70 to 80, or even 85, during a positive trend. In a very strong positive trend we might see RSI rise above 90 and stay there for a considerable period of time.

Absolutely Critical

An oscillator that maintains an overbought reading for a considerable time illustrates just how strong the underlying trend really is. The tool provides a partial signal, but the value of that partial signal may be greater than that of a full signal.

Stochastic Oscillator

George Lane, an analyst who extended the Williams percentage R indicator in the 1950s, also introduced the stochastic oscillator. This oscillator can be expressed by two lines on a chart, and it is also measured in readings between 0 and 100.

Stochastics, as they are sometimes called, come in two forms: fast and slow, with the fast stochastic oscillator represented by the symbol %K and the slow stochastic oscillator represented by %D.

The fast part of the stochastic oscillator, %K, compares the price of the stock to its highs and lows over a period of time. (Lane uses a default 14-day period, but other periods are also options.) The slow portion of the stochastic oscillator, %D, smooths the %K reading by applying a simple moving average. %D trails %K. A %K overall reading above 80 indicates overbought conditions; a reading below 20 suggests oversold conditions.

The stochastic oscillator offers signals when %K and %D intersect. When %K crosses above %D, we get a buy signal. When %K crosses below %D, we get a sell signal. These signals may occur within the borders of overbought or oversold conditions, though they typically occur when conditions are extended. Signals are valid for different time periods, depending on the chart period. The daily chart offers short-term signals, the weekly chart provides intermediate-term signals, and the monthly chart yields long-term signals.

Stochastic oscillator signals also commonly provide signals that confirm a chart pattern or reversal. Figure 5.2 shows the confirmation of the buy and sell on Kohl's Corp. (KSS) signals between the instrument's price movement and the oscillator. Divergences do occur from time to time, as noted on the chart. Occasionally these divergences can lead to stronger signals and predict a security's movement with relative accuracy.

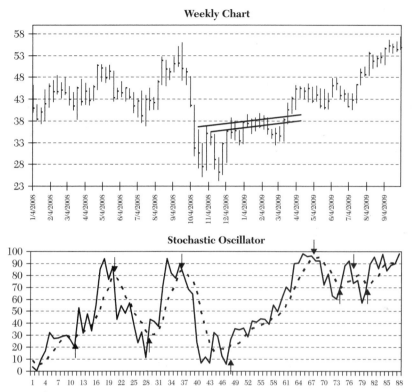

Figure 5.2 Weekly chart on Kohl's Corp. (KSS) showing the stochastic oscillators with buy and sell signals.

Commodity Channel Index

Developed by Donald Lambert, the commodity channel index (CCI) compares the price of a commodity to a simple moving average, then divides that measurement by the mean deviation. The CCI was built for commodities, though some managers use or adapt this indicator to work with securities.

The CCI has a range that exceeds the –100 to +100 zone, with positive movements above the zero line and negative movements below it. A reading above +100 shows an overbought condition; a reading below –100 shows an oversold condition.

Bollinger Bands

Named for and by founder John Bollinger, this indicator shows the boundaries of movement based on the volatility of an investment's price movement. Unlike other oscillators, Bollinger Bands are a price chart overlay, and do not have special scales.

Bollinger determined that an investment's normal price movement should remain within two standard deviations of a smoothed price movement. A simple moving average, usually 20 periods long, generally smooths price movement, though some technicians use an exponential moving average. The chart then paints lines on either side of that moving average, but two standard deviations away from it, producing what look like envelopes around the security's price. This is a very popular indicator among technicians, some of whom even use Bollinger Bands on other technical indicators.

Bollinger Bands provide information beyond indicating overbought and oversold investments. Differences between the bands converge and expand, based on the stock's movement over a period of time. This shows price volatility. Expanding distance between lines demonstrates

utmost crucial (handwritten note in left margin)

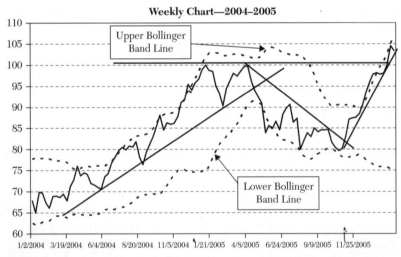

Weekly Chart—2004–2005

Upper Bollinger Band Line

Lower Bollinger Band Line

1/2/2004 3/19/2004 6/4/2004 8/20/2004 11/5/2004 1/21/2005 4/8/2005 6/24/2005 9/9/2005 11/25/2005

Figure 5.3 A weekly chart on FedEx Corp. (FDX) with the Bollinger Band overlay. In general, once a stock crosses a Bollinger Band, the price movement will likely retrace toward the moving average. This is an indication that the stock has moved outside its volatility zone of two sigma. In many instances, the movement retraces to the opposing Bollinger Band.

increasing volatility; converging lines show contracting volatility. This can be very helpful for analysts considering price movement expectations and their effect on the price of options contracts.

I often combine Bollinger Bands with other oscillators, looking for trend confirmations. When a stock price crosses above the upper Bollinger Band and the RSI or stochastic oscillator confirms an over-bought reading, it's much more likely that shares will reverse, moving lower for a short period of time. This may provide an opportunity to sell calls against the stock. By doing this just ahead of the price reversal, a manager can maximize the opportunity to generate income while still holding the position.

Let's look at an example of income generation on an overbought stock. Wal-Mart Stores (WMT) closed at $54.15 on November 18. There were several overbought readings on the daily chart. The 14-day relative strength index indicated an overbought condition, as did the Bollinger Bands indicator. A client who had purchased shares at the beginning of the month at $50.28 had an unrealized short-term gain of $3.47 per share, or 7.7 percent. Expecting that the stock would move higher in several weeks, we suggested selling a one-month call with a $55 strike price for $1.05. This generated income of $105,000 against the 100,000 purchased shares. The client's fund was willing to sell the shares at an effective price of $56.05 (strike price plus option premium) should the shares be called away. That would have generated a total profit of $577,000, or 11.5 percent.

It's also possible to combine Bollinger Bands with reversal patterns—those outlined in Chapter 4, as well as those associated with Japanese candlesticks.

CHAPTER 6

Oscillators and Strategies

OSCILLATOR SIGNALS PRESENT A VARIETY of strategic choices. Portfolio managers whose funds allow trading could sell shares on the confirmation of a short-term negative oscillator signal—though this could also mean losing out on upside participation, should the stock suddenly turn higher.

But many funds have provisions that prohibit them from trading their positions, especially core positions. Taxes and transaction charges may also keep managers from trading fund holdings. These funds and their managers may need or desire to employ options strategies if they are to make the best use of oscillator readings.

A stock that is in a positive trend and has reached overbought oscillator readings, for example, is likely a candidate for covered call overwriting. This is especially true if the overbought readings concur on the daily and weekly charts. Writing out-of-the money calls with between three and nine weeks to expiration can help to offset the anticipated share price decline during the correction phase.

Shares of Procter & Gamble (PG) rose to a high of $61.61, encountering resistance at a previous high. Furthermore, a test of the upper Bollinger Bands line showed overbought readings, as did the RSI, on both the daily and weekly charts.

A two-month call with a $65 strike price was trading at $2.00. In effect, a share owner could sell that contract and assume an obligation to sell the shares for an effective price of $67 if the option were called on a break above $65. If the shares remained below the $65 strike price and the contract expired worthless, the holder would realize a $2.00 per share profit, or 3.2 percent of the underlying share price, just for allowing time to pass.

Covered call overwriting allows the manager to profit from value decline, and also from time's movement. In some overbought situations, a consolidation or positive continuation phase may yield a sideways movement or slight correction. Neither produces a meaningful downward trend, but both may take a while to play out. (This situation is particularly likely when oscillators read "overbought" on the daily chart, but not on the weekly chart.) Consider writing short-term calls with between 15 and 45 days to expiration to benefit from sideways share price movements and the deterioration of time value. Your selection may depend on an issue's volatility and option premiums.

Option premiums generally deteriorate as expiration nears. Figure 6.1 shows the parabolic options time decay curve, based on an at-the-money option contract, from creation to death. The contract's value loss accelerates during the final month of the contract's life.

When option premiums (and therefore implied volatility levels) are low, portfolio managers may purchase put contracts to offset an anticipated significant decline. They might spot that potential decline by searching for overbought readings and subsequent negative signals on at least the weekly chart, and preferably on both the weekly and daily charts.

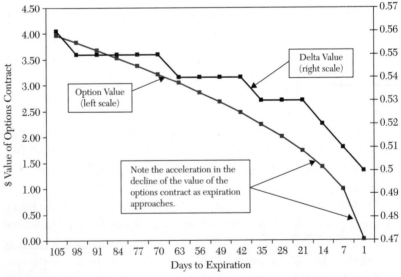

Figure 6.1 Graphic illustration of the at-the-money options parabolic time decay curve.

Consider purchasing a put contract that is slightly out-of-the-money with at least four weeks until expiration.

When oscillators show overbought conditions on the monthly chart, a different strategy may be in order. This is especially true if the overbought readings are concurrent on the monthly and weekly charts. Such readings can result in substantial and/or prolonged declines, or a prolonged period of sideways movement. Consider overwriting call options with between four and six months until expiration, or swapping the stock holding for a long-term call option, then writing calls against that position. This frees capital for other opportunities. *[margin handwriting: utmost crucial]*

Over a nine-month period, shares of Texas Instruments (TXN) rose to $25.44 from $14.35, a gain of 77.3 percent. A fund purchased the shares at $17.80 following the breakout and had an unrealized profit of 42.9 percent.

Not wanting to chance an erosion before year end, and with the oscillators giving overbought readings, the manager decided to sell a five-month call with a $27 strike price for $1.40. The option, which was 9.6 percent out of the money, generated a premium equivalent to 5.5 percent of the stock price. This provided some cushion against a short-term decline and helped the manager control market risk and performance.

The decision was likely a wise one. When oscillators give an oversold reading during an overall negative trend, countertrend movements may affect short positions. Shares in short-sale positions can be purchased against a fund manager's wishes.

Technical Indicators

In addition to oscillators, managers can also use other tools to evaluate the technical condition of a stock, index, ETF, currency, or any other vehicle. These tools can help judge trends and their strength. In this section we will examine some of these tools, from momentum to directional strength.

The momentum indicator is simple to calculate and use. It compares the latest price of a tradable instrument to the price during past time periods. (The default is 10 periods.) The indicator plots momentum on a separate scale, with both positive and negative values centered on the zero line. Zero indicates flat momentum. Many analysts plot momentum as a histogram, as shown in Figure 6.2. *[margin handwriting: crucial]*

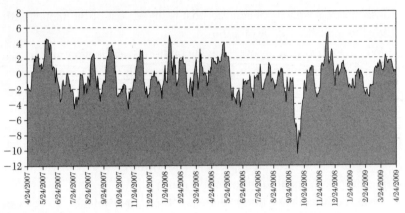

Figure 6.2 Daily momentum gauge histogram on Cemex SAB de C.V., April 2007–April 2009.

In many cases, momentum readings will show change before the trend actually changes. As a positive trend persists, momentum should expand, because more investors are buying. In a negative trend, momentum should also expand, as more and more investors sell off positions. Short selling may also expand negative momentum.

Momentum is slowing when readings begin to retreat back toward the zero line. This is the precursor to a trend change, potentially your first warning that a trend may become exhausted, well before it actually reaches its end. Such knowledge can help you plan to close a position, take an opposing position, or initiate one of the strategies discussed earlier.

Use a momentum indicator on any of the popular time periods. This technique offers particularly good trend indicators when used on a monthly chart.

The directional momentum indicators (DMI) and the average directional momentum index (ADX) are also useful tools for measuring momentum. Developed by J. Welles Wilder, DMI is comprised of two lines: one positive, one negative, and typically identified as +DI and –DI.

These lines, plotted above the zero line, show the momentum of positive and negative movements. The dominant trend has a positive reading, above the zero line, and the out-of-favor trend is below the zero line. The lines grow apart when the trend is expanding and move toward each other as the trend loses momentum.

Signals occur when the two lines cross. The reading is positive when the +DI line crosses above the –DI line, negative when the –DI line crosses above the +DI line. On a daily chart these are short-term signals, on weekly charts they are intermediate-term signals, and on monthly charts they are long-term signals. Weak or false signals are common, so use care and monitor new signals for confirmation.

At times, the lines appear intertwined. This is a neutral reading. DMI readings can change relatively frequently, based on trends' quick changes. Sustained trends create lines that grow further and further apart, indicating the trend's strength and longevity.

A third line, the average directional momentum index, also shows and confirms a prevailing trend's strength. As its name implies, ADX is an average of the readings from +DMI and –DMI. The stronger and longer the prevailing trend, the higher the ADX reading. ADX readings are the same for positive and negative trends. Readings below 22 indicate a neutral reading, while a cross above 22 confirms a new trend.

Figure 6.3 shows the stock of Deere & Co. (DE). Notice three lines on the bottom section of the chart. These are +DMI, –DMI, and ADX.

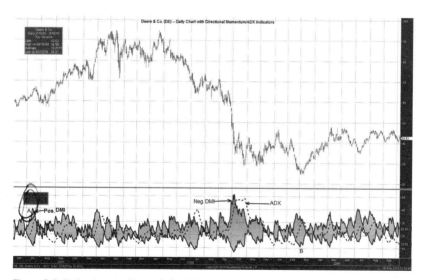

Figure 6.3 Daily chart on Deere & Co. (DE) showing the directional momentum indicators and the Average Directional Momentum Index (ADX). Chart courtesy of Bloomberg Professional Service.

Then note the negative signal (point A) on the DMI chart. This is the first indication that a new trend is beginning.

ADX still has a positive reading at point A, because it is a lagging indicator. As the DMI's negative reading expands, the ADX declines, exhausting possible positive readings. When ADX turns higher (point B), it confirms the negative DMI readings. In other words, the negative trend has continued long enough to become the prevailing trend.

ADX is perhaps best used to confirm the beginning of a consolidation pattern. As we noted in Chapter 4, pennant, flags, and other continuation and consolidation patterns eventually resolve. On its way, the pattern usually—but not always—retests the breakout point, giving managers another opportunity to enter a position.

During consolidation patterns, as there is little or no trend, ADX readings are usually below 22. The longer the consolidation, the lower the ADX reading. Readings below 10 can indicate that a sideways trend has existed for a while. When ADX rises back above 22, it confirms a new, potentially sustainable trend.

These patterns can help managers buy options while premiums are low. Option premiums are generally low in sideways markets, regardless of which way the market ultimately heads. Neutral and narrowing trends generally bring cheaper contract prices, because they push volatility low for a long time.

A low ADX reading indicates low volatility, as do intertwined DMI lines and narrowing trend lines. An overlay of Bollinger Band lines should show lines converging as the standard deviation measurement declines as well. At this point, a call or put purchase may be very inexpensive.

During periods of narrowing consolidation, many investors consider purchasing combinations, also known as straddles or strangles. This is especially true before binary events, such as a new product release or an upcoming earnings announcement, that could move a stock higher or lower. The risk/reward ratio can be very favorable.

Relative Performance

Technical analysis can help investors judge the strength of a stock, an index, an exchange traded fund, or any other instrument relative to a benchmark such as the S&P 500 Index (SPX), the Russell 2000 Index

(RUT), the Wilshire 6000 Index (WSX), or the S&P Supercomposite 1500 Index (SPUPR).

Two different methods produce the same result. The first—and least complicated—method is to divide the price of the stock by its relevant benchmark.

The second, slightly more complicated computation involves dividing a stock's daily return by the daily return of its benchmark. I modify this formula slightly to show more perspective on relative performance. I look at a stock's relative performance over 14 daily periods, then divide the 14-day performance by the relevant index's 14-day performance. This indicator can offer great opportunities to create alpha. As you read the chart, look at the formation and trend, not at relative performance numbers' actual numerical readings.

almost critical

Figure 6.4 shows relative performance—not to be confused with the RSI oscillator—computed by the first method and plotted on a lower pane of the chart. Johnson & Johnson (JNJ) has shown both positive and weak relative performance over the year. Overlay this stock chart with the SPX chart to see how the stock moved in comparison to SPX.

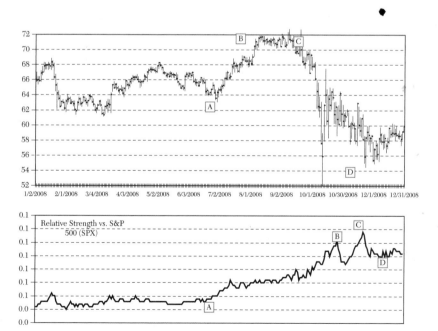

Figure 6.4 Daily chart on Johnson & Johnson (JNJ) with relative performance/ strength versus the S&P 500 Index (SPX), 2008.

Notice the strength (between point A and point B) and weakness (point C to point D). A manager who purchased JNJ shortly after point A and held the shares until point B would have outperformed the SPX. A manager who purchased shares between points C and D would have underperformed the SPX. An investor who sold shares short between points C and D would have outperformed the SPX if the stock had been in a negative trend.

Neutral relative performance means that stock and benchmark returns are equivalent. Owning the stock would give nearly the same result as owning the S&P Depository Receipts (SPY), commonly referred to as SPiDRs, which offers performance that's virtually equivalent to the SPX.

Finding the Strongest or Weakest Stocks

To locate the strongest and weakest stocks, we can search sectors, then industry groups, to find the strongest and weakest performers within them.

Or search for winners and losers on the relative performance percentile, which lets analysts see relative performance over any time period they construct. Figure 6.5 shows the strongest and weakest stocks, in order, with their sectors.

Knowing both the leaders and the laggards can be very profitable, particularly when a sector begins to outperform its neighbors. Watch for laggards to make their moves and stay on the lookout for reversal or breakout patterns in those issues, while continuing to look for movement on the relative performance percentile charts.

The pairs trade can also help managers profit from relative performance information. In a pairs trade, an investor purchases one stock and sells another against it. Other strategies, such as long calls, long puts, naked writes, or spreads, can increase the profit potential and minimize the risk associated with this strategy.

Pairs ideas can also be used on sectors, market capitalization groupings, or indices. Let's look at an example of relative performance between two sectors and set up an appropriate pairs trade.

A commodities-driven bull market, such as that of 2009, provides a good backdrop. Following a 14-month decline, the basic materials sector began an upside breakout with positive performance relative to the S&P

Ticker	Short Name	Incl. Sector	Real YTD Return
None (2916 securities)			
MMR US Equity	MCMORAN EXPLORAT	Energy	101.69
CPE US Equity	CALLON PETROLEUM	Energy	99.67325
EXXI US Equity	ENERGY XXI BERMU	Energy	72.76069
WNC US Equity	WABASH NATIONAL	Consumer, Cyclical	69.98109
CNXT US Equity	CONEXANT SYS.	Technology	69.94779
PCYC US Equity	PHARMACYCLICS	Consumer, Non-cyclical	64.43234
ZIGO US Equity	ZYCO CORP.	Industrial	64.13176
LAB US Equity	LABRANCHE & CO.	Financial	63.82377
RUTH US Equity	RUTH'S HOSPITALI	Consumer, Cyclical	63.72337
MAPP US Equity	MAP PHARMACEUTIC	Consumer, Non-cyclical	62.09669
MSPD US Equity	MINDSPEED TECHNO	Technology	61.90872
BARE US Equity	BARE ESCENTUALS	Consumer, Non-cyclical	64.79677
CDII US Equity	CHINA DIRECT IND	Consumer, Non-cyclical	63.80801
SIRI US Equity	SIRIUS XM RADIO	Communications	61.69222
ZION US Equity	ZIONS BANCORP	Financial	60.0779
EK US Equity	EASTMAN KODAK	Industrial	48.06603
PVTB US Equity	PRIVATE BAN CORP	Financial	47.68044
SSYS US Equity	STRATASYS INC.	Technology	46.26688
BBEP US US Equity	BRETTEURN ENERGY	Energy	43.64662
VCI US Equity	VALASSIS. COMM.	Consumer, Non-cyclical	43.09309
PRXL US Equity	PAREXEL INTL	Consumer, Non-cyclical	42.70027
IDIX US Equity	IDENIX PHARM.	Consumer, Non-cyclical	41.66288
ACAS US Equity	AMERICAN CAPITAL	Financial	41.49786
LYV US Equity	LIVE NATION ENTE.	Consumer, Non-cyclical	40.83226
WTNY US Equity	WHITNEY HLDG	Financial	40.83106
DPZ US Equity	DOMINO'S PIZZA	Consumer, Cyclical	39.40736
VDSI US Equity	VASCO DATA INTL	Communications	38.1896
SGI US Equity	SILICON GRAPHICS	Technology	37.78686
NFP US Equity	NATIONAL FINANCI	Financial	38.63976
LCC US Equity	US AIRWAYS GROUP	Consumer, Cyclical	36.66645
MNI US Equity	MCCLATCHY CO-A	Communications	36.63962
TASR US Equity	TASER INTL.	Industrial	36.26616
RICK US Equity	RICKS CABARET	Consumer, Cyclical	36.25736
ARAY US Equity	ACCURAY INC.	Industrial	34.98498
WBS US Equity	WEBSTER FINL.	Financial	34.97486
HBAN US Equity	HUNTINGTON BANC	Financial	34.67836
SUSQ US Equity	SUSQUBHAN ENCSHS	Financial	34.23496
SFN US Equity	SPHERION CORP.	Consumer, Non-cyclical	34.22612
ARG US Equity	AIRGAS INC.	Basic Materials	33.90029
LXK US Equity	LEXMARK INTL-A	Technology	33.6162
IVAC US Equity	INTEVAC INC.	Industrial	33.31699
SBGI US Equity	SINCLAIR BROAD-A	Communications	33.295
CROX US Equity	CROCS INC.	Consumer, Cyclical	33.14962
MEI US Equity	METHODE ELEC.	Industrial	32.76666
ATV US Equity	ACORN INTERN-ADR	Communications	32.63331
MEI US Equity	MBIA INC.	Financial	32.3488
LCAV US Equity	LCA-VISION INC.	Consumer, Non-cyclical	32.21674
FRZ US Equity	REDDY ICE HOLD	Industrial	32.02684
TSN US Equity	TYSON FOODS-A	Consumer, Non-cyclical	31.76462
MHO US Equity	MM HOMES INC.	Consumer, Cyclical	31.11106
FNSR US Equity	FINSAR CORP.	Communications	31.08484
SNV US Equity	SYNOVUS FINL	Financial	31.01924
GNW US Equity	GENWORTH FINANCI	Financial	30.86669
CEN US Equity	CIENA CORP.	Communications	30.86434
NKTR US Equity	NEKTAR THERAPEUT	Consumer, Non-cyclical	30.8309
ALOC US Equity	AUDIO-CODES LTD.	Communications	30.69243
CFL US Equity	BRINKS HOME SECU	Consumer, Non-cyclical	30.16963
BZQ US Equity	PROSHARES ULTRA	Funds	30.16804
KEY US Equity	KEY CORP.	Financial	29.49061
SANM US Equity	SANMINA-SCI CORP.	Industrial	29.36664
ALKS US Equity	ALKERMIES INC.	Consumer, Non-cyclical	28.91451
CHRD US Equity	CHORDIANT SOFTWR	Communications	28.87163
APKT US Equity	ACME PACKET INC	Communications	28.67639
EDZ US Equity	EMER MKT BEAR 3X	Funds	28.34618
KLIC US Equity	KULICKE & SOFFA	Technology	28.3029
AMLN US Equity	AMYLIN PHARM INC.	Consumer, Non-cyclical	28.04938
WAL US Equity	WESTERN ALLIANCE	Financial	27.89973
AFFX US Equity	AFFY METRIX INC.	Consumer, Non-cyclical	27.70411
LEN US Equity	LENNAR CORP.-CLA	Consumer, Cyclical	27.66733
SJT US Equity	SAN JUAN BASIN	Energy	27.63366
DRV US Equity	DIREXION DAI-EEA	Funds	27.63109

Figure 6.5 Relative year-to-date performance of options stocks, showing the strongest stocks.

500 Index (SPX) and rising momentum. The utilities sector, by contrast, stayed weak relative to SPX.

The bull market was moving higher, so we sought to buy the outperforming sector and sell the underperforming sector. To show the relationship between the two sectors we graphed the Select Sector SPiDR—Basic Materials ETF (XLB) against the Select Sector SPiDR—Utilities ETF (XLU), shown in Figure 6.6—Relative performance between Basic Materials (XLB) ETF and Utilities (XLU) ETF on a daily chart. When XLB is outperforming XLU the line rises, compared to the line declining when XLU outperforms XLB.

The rising line indicates that the numerator (XLB) is rising in relation to the denominator (XLU). This chart lets us monitor performance and provides signals when the performance relationship may be peaking or turning.

At the beginning of April, XLB was at $23. We purchased a 2-1/2 month call with a $24 strike price for $1.04. At the same time, with XLU at $25.50, we sold the $24 strike puts at $0.63.

At the June expiration XLB was at $26.07 and XLU was at $27.47. We realized a $1.03 profit in the calls; the puts expired worthless for a gain of $0.63 and a total profit of $1.66 per share. Managers could also have closed the position for a larger profit on a double-top reversal.

Absolutely critical (handwritten margin note)

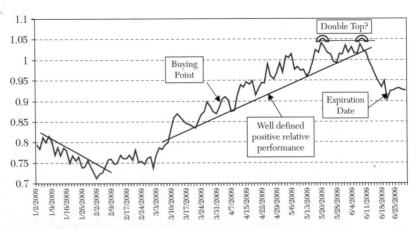

Figure 6.6 Daily Chart for Basic Materials (XLB) vs. Utilities (XLU).

Money Flow and On-Balance Volume

Money flow shows the passage of funds from buyers to sellers. Money flow should increase in bullish markets as more investors commit capital. Conversely, money flow should ebb when investors sell their holdings or sell shares short, providing capital to buyers or short-sale repurchasers.

Measure money flow by multiplying a stock's daily volume by the average of the day's high, low, and closing prices. Analysts add positive money flow (which occurs when stocks end higher) to the previous session's readings, and subtract negative money flow (which occurs when stocks end lower) from the previous session's total.

The on-balance volume (OBV) indicator is very much like money flow, but without price averages. Invented by Joseph Granville, the OBV is a running volume total with daily readings added to or subtracted from the overall balance according to whether shares moved higher or lower. It can also confirm trend changes, which in turn suggest a variety of strategies.

Money flow and OBV logically rise during accumulation phases and fall during distribution phases. When shares turn lower as money flow and OBV weaken, it confirms a trend change. An increase in implied volatility may also occur, driving up option premiums and making covered call overwriting a potentially profitable strategy. Alternatively, an investor could sell both the shares and some out-of-the-money put contracts, planning to repurchase the stock after share prices decline below the put's strike price.

When money flow and OBV weaken during an accumulation phase, a negative divergence begins. This may be an early indication that cash is no longer flowing into the security. The trend may be changing, making this a good time to plan a covered call overwriting strategy.

A covered combination strategy also lets managers take advantage of higher volatility levels. To execute the strategy, managers use a margin account to purchase between one-quarter and one-half of the manager's normal position in the underlying shares, then write an equivalent number of out-of-the-money calls and out-of-the-money puts.

This strategy combines the characteristics of covered call writing and naked put writing. Investors profit when the share price rises above the call strike price and shares are called away, generating what should be an attractive return. If the stock remains unchanged, managers continue to hold the stock while capturing the option premiums. If the stock price drops below the put contract's exercise price, the manager buys the remaining one-half or one-quarter of the position, depending on the number of contracts sold, yielding a lower average purchase price than that offered by the stock's original value.

For an example of a covered combination in action, assume that, as managers, we would normally purchase 100,000 shares of stock. For our example, we will purchase a half position or 50,000 shares of XYZ at $65.34. We'll sell 500 two-month calls with a $70 strike at $1.60, plus 500 two-month puts with a $60 strike at $1.65 for a net debit of $62.09.

Excluding transaction charges, the capital requirement—based on the industry minimum margin requirement—is $1,939,900. Interest charges total $0.26 per share, based on a 5 percent annual rate calculated to expiration.

If shares rise above the $70 strike price and are called, the strategy generates a profit of $382,341.25, or 19.7 percent. If the stock remains unchanged at $65.34 at expiration, the strategy generates a profit from the sale of the two options, yielding $149,341.25, or 7.7 percent. If the stock price drops below the put's $60 strike and the contract was assigned, the fund purchases another 50,000 shares, creating an average cost of $61.18 per share, 6.4 percent below the original purchase price of the stock.

The covered combination is one of my favorite strategies, because it provides opportunities for success over a wide range of prices. A security can rise sharply, rise moderately, change relatively little, fall moderately, or drop sharply. In four out of those five scenarios, the covered combination makes money (though one scenario involves limited upside potential). A stock position, by contrast, profits only if the stock rises moderately or sharply. The covered combination strategy greatly increases the probability of success.

It also helps the fund benefit from the options premium decay during the holding period and lets investors take advantage of higher volatility levels. Professionals refer to this practice as "selling gamma" or "selling volatility," a form of strategic investing that relies on collecting premiums.

CHAPTER 7

Relative
Performance

IN THE LATE 1980s and early 1990s, the American Stock Exchange (ASE) introduced S&P Depository Receipts (SPY), now more commonly known as SPiDRs, and many other products, which are classified as Exchange Traded Funds.

Like a mutual fund, SPY is a basket of stocks. When they buy shares in it, investors effectively purchase shares in the entire S&P 500 Index (SPX). SPY shares are approximately 1/10th of SPX. Unlike a mutual fund, however, investors can trade SPY all day long, taking new positions and closing old ones as market conditions change. SPY became a template for a slate of other exchange-traded funds (ETFs), an investment type that has made it easier for both small and large investors to trade easily and efficiently in whole markets, market sectors, and other asset classes.

In addition to offering new trading products, ETFs' introduction also provided new market analysis tools. We have briefly discussed the use of relative strength and performance information. It's obvious that finding the strongest stocks and holding positions in those shares should provide the best performance. It is also evident that the strongest stock(s) *should* fall within the strongest industry groups, and that the strongest industry groups are likely within the strongest sectors. Top-down technical analysis helps analysts find the strongest and weakest stocks, industries, and sectors. ETF analysis helps by identifying relative performance.

ETF services cover a varying number of sectors with their funds, from about nine to around 15. I use Select Sector SPiDR ETFs, which represent nine of the major sectors; I add two others to round out the bunch.

crucial

(Because I produce a weekly chart book, I have created programs that include other industry groups I think are important to the market.)

The most important 11 sectors that I follow using ETFs are:

utmost crucial

Select Sector SPiDR—Consumer Discretionary
Select Sector SPiDR—Consumer Nondiscretionary (staples)
Select Sector SPiDR—Energy
Select Sector SPiDR—Financial
Select Sector SPiDR—Health Care
Select Sector SPiDR—Industrial
Select Sector SPiDR—Materials (commodity related)
Select Sector SPiDR—Technology (communications included)
Select Sector SPiDR—Utility
SPiDR S&P Retail Sector ETF
iSHARES DJ US Transportation Average

The growing importance and impact of the real estate market has recently made the iSHARES DJ Real Estate Index Fund (IYR) a popular and important selection as well.

very cruc

For broad market representation I use SPY, the PowerShares NASDAQ 100 Trust (QQQQ), and the iSHARES Russell 2000 Index Fund (IWM).

As I select ETFs, I look for liquidity, trade activity, and options that trade against a given fund. Less-traded funds yield inferior analysis results. Every week I look closely at these instruments' individual charts and decide if they are positive, negative, or neutral, based on their own merits. I compare them against each other, using relative performance analysis, then compare positive and negative charts against their peers.

utmost cruc

By drilling down, I find the best of the best and the worst of the worst. Before acting on this information, I also check momentum indicators. Changing momentum is usually an early indication that one trend is ending and another, reverse trend may be beginning.

Before I suggest leveraged trades, I also check to make certain I'm using appropriate ETFs. Several ETF issuers have created leveraged versions of some of the most popular funds. These funds have titles that include phrases such as "double performance," "triple short," and so on, meaning that their performance should be two, three, four, or more times regular funds' performance. Other funds have inverse properties and may be called "short" or bearish funds.

Both fund types would seem to offer possibilities for increased returns, but in many cases they don't always work that way. Many of these funds use over-the-counter derivatives or other products as their investment vehicles and are re-balanced on a daily basis. Rebalancing wipes out most of their gains and losses from previous sessions, making them a good bet for intraday hedging and trading, but poor longer-term investment tools.

Consider the Select Sector SPiDR—Financial (XLF) fund, which lost 59.3 percent during 2008, part of the bear market in financial stocks. Over the same period, the Ultra-short Financial ETF was little changed. The fund's description suggested that investors should have realized a return of approximately 90 percent or more. In fact, one week before the end of 2008, the ultra-short fund had a loss. Don't rely on leveraged ETF funds for long-term gains. Consider using long put or call options for leverage, plus other strategies for producing income.

Look at the Board

Figure 7.1 shows a screenshot of 12 ETFs. A side-by-side look at the group lets us see which sectors and funds are performing best and worst; it also gives an overall sense of the market. Each of the charts offers graphs depicting price, momentum, and relative performance versus the S&P 1500 Supercomposite Index (SPUPR). Together, these three data sets provide a great amount of comparative information about these funds.

Consider price first. If all the trends are pointing higher, the general trend should be up. If the trends are all pointing lower, the general trend should be down. This quick, comparative view can show which—if any—sectors are diverging from the rest, narrowing the search for best- and worst-performing groups.

Momentum adds two more important pieces of information. First, it shows whether a trend is accelerating or decelerating. It's usually most profitable to trade during rising trends with increasing momentum, because there is apparently a feeling of unlimited upside potential. (Accelerating negative momentum indicates that a downward movement is likely to continue and also presents opportunities to make money.)

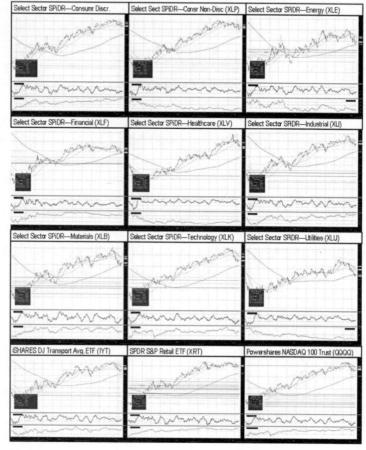

Figure 7.1 This is a layout with 12 ETFs that I monitor for relative performance and momentum.

Second, momentum indicators can show that a trend is waning, which may indicate an upcoming trend change. In many instances a change in momentum direction that crosses the zero line is the first indication of a trend reversal.

Relative performance shows how a fund is performing versus the broad market. In this case, the broad market is the S&P Supercomposite Index (SPUPR), which provides a very broad trading overview, one that incorporates every sector's performance. Some sectors will lead the market; others will lag overall performance, with new sectors replacing older ones as a trend continues.

When the best and worst sectors in a bull market change, managers may want to exit positions in the original leading sectors, write calls against those holdings, or purchase protective put contracts.

In a bear market, managers often look for the fastest-declining sectors, then sell shares short or purchase puts on stocks in those sectors as they lead the market lower. To find these sectors, look for negative relative performance, recalling that once again, there will be leading and lagging sectors. Short or equivalent short positions in the leading groups will likely provide better relative returns.

As negative sectors begin to turn higher, managers might purchase calls or write puts to protect those positions. Consider repurchasing shares or closing options strategies. By purchasing or shorting positions in leading sectors, managers typically create alpha, or returns that beat their relative benchmarks. Alpha generates earned performance compensation and attracts new capital. By using derivative product strategies, managers use leverage and volatility to create alpha without incurring additional risk. Traders compare implied volatility (based on option premiums) with realized or historic volatility (based on the underlying security's movements in either direction over time).

CHAPTER 8

ETF Strategies

ETFS ARE BASKETS OF STOCKS, usually with shares from at least 15 companies. They not only represent a certain group or broader sector, but also offer diversification's smoothing effects. An ETF typically produces returns that are between those of the group's best and worst components.

Overall, ETFs are generally less volatile than the most volatile stock in the mix and may have very short periods when overall volatility is at or even below that of the least volatile stock in the represented group, usually because of the ETF's own trading patterns. In many cases it is better to purchase ETF options than to write them, because of these generally lower volatility levels.

Sharp declines, however, may mean higher volatility for ETFs. The bear market of 2007 to 2009, for instance, produced high levels of volatility and increased option premiums. Several strategies may help managers adjust for these increased levels.

The simple bull or bear spread strategy is first. An investor who writes an out-of-the-money contract versus the option he or she wants to purchase reduces the risk of inflated premiums and higher costs.

Consider XYZ, a hypothetical ETF on the technology sector, with shares trading strongly at $15.72. Market conditions put implied volatility around 40 percent, compared to a 52-week low of 18.2 percent. With risk premiums nearly more than double their lows, buying a seven-week, at-the-money call with a $15 strike costs $1.50. The 30-day realized volatility is 31.1 percent and the sigma of the 20-day moving average is around 0.65. The 30-day realized volatility reading represents the movement of the underlying shares over a 30-day trading period.

Some may find this option expensive. Those investors might purchase the option and write a call with the same expiration period, an $18 strike, and a price of $0.45, creating a spread for a $1.05 net debit. The limited downside risk, if XYZ falls below the $15 strike and the options expire, is $1.05 per share, or 100 percent of the investment. (The ultimate loss would total $15.72 per share if the ETF drops to zero, which is unlikely.) However, a drop below the $14.67 level would result in a greater capital loss.

The upside potential is realized if XYZ rises above $18, an increase of 14.5 percent during the holding period. That would mean a maximum spread value of $3.00 per share for a gain of $1.95 per share: a return of 185.7 percent. A 14.5 percent gain for any instrument in this time frame is unusual, but can occur when volatility is high and momentum is strong. The manager forfeits any appreciation above $18.

If the fund moves about 15 percent from its current market price, we might use a different, slightly more risky slant on this strategy. As an alternative to purchasing one option and selling one contract against it, a manager could buy one option and sell two contracts against it, dropping the debit cost from $1.05 to $0.60 per share.

The maximum downside risk is to the debit cost of $0.60 per share. The point of maximum profit—where the long call is worth the most while the short call is simultaneously worth zero—happens when XYZ's price is $18. In this case the spread has a theoretical worth of $3 per share for a profit of $2.40, or 400 percent of the debit cost. (The actual capital requirement will be higher due to the naked options margin requirement; the spread is only partially covered.)

Each point above the $18 strike price means one point offset against the gain, until the short call eats the entire profit and liability exceeds benefit. In this case, that point comes if and when the ETF rises above $20.40. This point is 29.8 percent above the XYZ's initial $15.72 value. Whether this strategy fits a portfolio's risk/reward profile is a managerial judgment call.

A third strategy might include the original $15/$18 call spread, plus selling seven-week puts with a $14 strike and $0.65 price to help finance the spread purchase. The trade's net debit is now $0.40 per share. This strategy also achieves maximum profit when XYZ reaches $18, closing the spread for its theoretical value of $3.00 and yielding a profit of $2.60 per share, or 650 percent of the net debit. The capital requirement for this strategy, once again, is greater, due to the naked put sale.

The break-even point comes when XYZ trades at $15.40, thirty-two cents below its current price. If XYZ's price moves above $18, no further gain is achieved. If the price of XYZ drops below the $14 strike price, we can assume that, at expiration, the manager will own the shares for an equivalent price of $14405 ($14.40 strike plus $0.40 net debit). The risk exposure at this point is equivalent to the risk of simply purchasing the shares outright.

Who should use each of these strategies? That depends on the manager, the fund's risk/reward profile, and the fund's ability to initiate various trade types. As a strategist, I consider several strategies, compare them, and look for the most appropriate fit. For these strategies, the comparison would look something like the chart shown in Table 8.1.

This chart indicates that, in this case, strategies two and four are the best alternatives, even compared to purchasing the shares outright. Higher premiums would have made other techniques possible, as in the next example.

ZYX is an example of an energy sector ETF in July 2009. At this time the shares were priced at $45.94, and a short-term positive

	Strategy #1 Long Call	Strategy #2 1:1 Bull Spread	Strategy #3 1:2 Bull Spread	Strategy #4 1:1 Bull Spread + Put Write	Strategy #5 Buy ETF Shares	Best
Net Debit	$1.50	$1.05	$0.60	$0.40	$15.72	#4
Capital Requirement	$1.50	$1.05	$2.62	$2.62	$15.72	#2
Max Profit at/ Profit	Unlimited	$18.00/ $1.95 or 185.7%	$18.00/ $2.40 or 91.7%	$18.00/ $2.60 or 99.2%	Unlimited	#1 or #5
Max Loss at/ Loss.	$15.00/ $1.50 or 100%	$15.00/ $1.05 or 100%	Upside – Unlimited Downside – $0.60 or 22.9%	$0 / $14.40	$0 / $15.72 or 100%	#2 or #3
Up Break-Even	n/a	n/a	$20.40		n/a	
Down Break-Even	$16.50	$16.05	$15.60	$15.40 and $14.40 (if put is assigned)	$15.72	#4

Table 8.1 Comparing different strategies that are looking for a positive move in ETF XYZ.

trend channel was developing. Momentum was on the rise and oscillators were positive, but not nearing overbought readings. Pricing data showed strong resistance near the $51 level, and relative performance showed that the ETF was moving up the leader board. Implied volatility was flat at around 48 percent, and historic volatility was at 56.7 percent.

Given these readings, I looked for alternatives to purchasing the shares. I first considered a covered call write: buying ZYX and selling a seven-week call with a $50 strike at $1.51 for a net trade debit of $44.43 per share. (This is also the capital requirement for a cash account purchase.)

The goal is for the ETF to rise above $50 with shares called away at the strike price. That would leave the investment fund with a profit of $5.57 per share, or 12.4 percent. The fund realizes no share gain if the share price remains unchanged at $45.94, but the call value would decline to zero, yielding a profit of $1.51 per share, or 3.4 percent. The downside break-even point is the debit price of $44.43, which is 3.3 percent below the stock's current market price. This difference acts as a risk buffer.

The second potential strategy is a bull spread using calls. As with the previous example using XYZ, purchase an at-the-money call with a $46 strike and sell against it a seven-week call with a $50 strike, giving a $1.42 debit. The manager earns maximum profit when the spread is at its theoretical full value: the difference between the strike prices, or $4.00 per share, which occurs with ZYX at $50 or higher. The maximum profit would be $2.58 per share, or 181.7 percent.

A maximum loss of $1.42, or 100 percent, occurs if the shares remain below the $46 strike price. The trade breaks even at the point where the hypothetical ZYX's price is equal to the sum of the debit price plus the lower strike price. That happens at $47.42, or 3.2 percent above the current share price.

Still another strategy involves selling out-of-the-money puts and taking advantage of the time premium. This strategy has limited upside potential, but does allow a fund to benefit from the passage of time, a practice traders refer to as "selling theta."

To do this, look for an out-of-the-money put contract, which provides some downside cushion, plus an option with less than two months to expiration to maximize the time-decay curve. In this case we'll consider seven-week options using a put with a strike price of $43 and a price of $2.02. This trade must be done in a margin account; the capital requirement, based on the industry minimum, is $6.25 per share. (Most firms have higher requirements.)

If the shares remain above $43 until expiration, the put expires worthless and the fund keeps the premium—$2.02, or 32.3 percent— as profit. If the shares drop below the $43 strike and the put is assigned, the fund pays an effective cost of $40.98 to own each share. That's 10.8 percent below the share price when the trade began and is also the downside break-even price.

The situation's higher implied volatility and option premiums suggest considering a covered combination, which combines covered call writing and put contract writing in one strategy. This allows us to take advantage of volatility, which traders refer to as "selling gamma."

Execute the covered combination by purchasing either a half or quarter share position, then selling equivalent amounts of out-of-the-money calls and puts. (To evaluate and compare strategies, we'll continue the one-share analysis.) Purchase the shares, then sell a seven-week call with a $50 strike for $1.51 and a put with a $42 strike for $1.76, giving a net trading debit of $42.67. This trade must occur in a margin account; the capital requirement, based on the industry minimum, is $26.71.

If the shares rise above the $50 strike price, the fund realizes a profit of $7.16 per share, or 26 percent. If ZYX remains at $45.94, the trade yields $3.10 per share, or 11.6 percent. If the share price drops below the put's $42 strike price and the put is assigned, the fund will then own twice as many shares, constituting a half or whole position with an average effective cost of $42.42 per share, or 7.7 percent below ZYX's price on the day we initiated the strategy. Omitting dividends and transaction charges, but including margin interest of 5 percent, gives a net cost of $0.17 per share.

As with our first example, let's compare these strategies to see which offer the lowest risks and highest rewards. (See Table 8.2.)

	Strategy #1 Covered Call	Strategy #2 1:1 Bull Spread	Strategy #3 Write Naked Put	Strategy #4 Covered Combination	Strategy #5 Buy ETF Shares	Best
Net Debit	$44.43	$1.42	$2.02 cr.	$42.67	$45.94	#2, #3
Capital Requirement°	$44.43	$1.42	$6.25	$26.71	$45.94	#2
Max Profit at/ Profit	$50 / $5.57 or 12.4%	$50 / $2.58 or 181.7%	$43 or above / $2.02 or 32.3%	$50 / $7.16 or 26.8%	Unlimited	#2 ?#5
Max Loss at/ Loss	Zero / $44.43 or 100%	$46 $1.42 or 100%	Zero / $40.98	Zero / $42.42	Zero / $45.94	#2
Up Break-Even	n/a	n/a	n/a	n/a	n/a	
Down Break-Even	$44.43 or 3.3% lower	$47.42 or 3.2% above	$40.98 or 10.8% lower	$42.42 or 7.7% lower	$45.94 -0-	#4

Table 8.2 Comparing different strategies.

The best overall strategy is likely number two, the bull call spread, as long as the strategy meets the risk/reward profile for the fund that pursues it. Strategy four provides both upside participation and an impressive downside risk buffer. Strategy three, the naked put, provides an attractive downside cushion, but no upward participation. Simply buying ETF shares is a choice with tremendous upside potential, but lots of downside risk.

Pairs

ETFs offer investors the option of taking sector positions and enjoying some diversification without buying individual stocks. ETFs also allow for efficient portfolio management without the need to closely monitor individual stocks.

Even so, managers may realize profits by tracking an ETF's individual securities. It's advantageous to know the trading status and company news, including product release dates, earnings announcements, and dividends of competitive corporations. Some funds are also tied to specific sectors, such as health care or biotechnology, and it's worthwhile to follow news about those industry groups. All these may provide trading opportunities.

We discussed the wisdom of looking at markets and sectors for strong and weak performers. We can use a similar process on an ETF's component stocks.

Let's look at the Select Sector SPiDR—Materials ETF (XLB), which included 29 stocks in July 2009. Each of these companies has different fundamentals, though some may be similar.

Figure 8.1 shows XLB's price movement, along with the momentum indicator and relative performance versus SPX. (I have removed other studies in order to keep the chart simple for this illustration.) Relative performance, in the bottom panel, shows some improvement; upward momentum is rising. This is partially because the recent overall market was strong, with other sectors leading it higher.

A line's movement is more important than its value, for our purposes. A rising relative performance or relative strength line shows outperformance; a declining line shows lagging or negative relative performance. In this case XLB is rising, slightly outperforming the S&P 500 index.

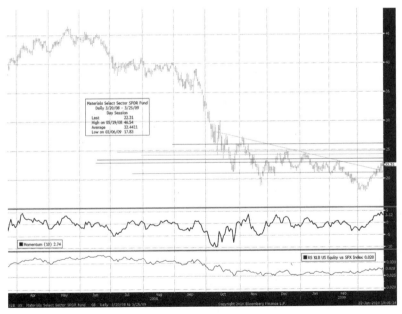

Figure 8.1 A Bloomberg LP chart on the Select Sector SPiDR—Materials Fund (XLB). Note how the shares are rising from their lows with strong upward momentum. Relative performance is improving.

Next, we'll identify the group's strongest and weakest stocks. Of the ETF's 29 component stocks, several have matched the market over the previous several weeks. Other have outperformed the market and are beginning to roll over; still others are beginning to outperform the market after lagging.

MeadWestvaco Corp. (MWV) was one of the strongest stocks over the previous two weeks, rising from a low with strong relative performance and good momentum. This is a stock that many managers might like to own. Momentum has been strong as well. Figure 8.2 shows MWV's data.

International Flavors & Fragrances (IFF) has also been a positive performer, but is beginning to roll over, with weakening relative performance and momentum that's turning lower. Many managers are watching this stock for a potential break.

Knowing the leaders and laggards can help managers form investment strategies. A manager who already owns XLB may overweight by taking a position on MWV or a negative position on IFF.

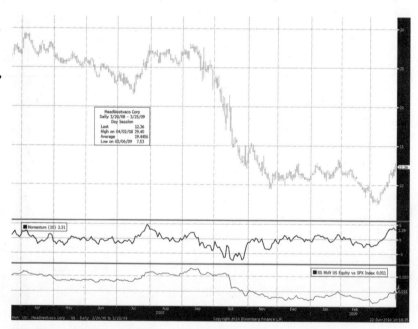

Figure 8.2 A Bloomberg LP chart on MeadWestvaco (MWV). Note that relative performance (bottom panel) is improving and momentum has been strong (middle panel).

Risk-averse managers would likely opt for the second idea, because the risk of being wrong on IFF would likely be partially offset by XLB's movement.

With IFF at $30.48, consider buying a seven-week bear spread using puts. Purchase the $30 strike at $1.55 and sell the $25 strike at $0.45 for a net debit of $1.10. The fund participates in the ETF's upside movement and benefits from any weakness as leadership changes. IFF's break-even price is $28.90, or 5.2 percent below the current share price. If the shares resume their positive move the spread will expire, but the $1.10 price could be offset by XLB's gains.

Another alternative, which some managers may find more palatable, would involve writing seven-week calls with a $30 strike on IFF, then trading at $2.55. Maximum profit occurs at a share price of $30 or lower, representing a decline of 1.6 percent, which would let a fund capture the $2.55 premium. The strategy's break-even point is IFF at $32.55 (strike price + premium received).

These trades, known as pairs, help investors benefit from the divergence of two tradable instruments. In this case, the sectors pair trade uses an ETF as the base and adds a stock that has led the fund higher but is now losing momentum.

A sector or industry group typically appreciates past the point at which its initial leaders begin to lose upward power, pushed by lagging stocks that often appreciate for longer than the leaders—though not necessarily for an extended time period. Managers usually have an opportunity to profit from a positive trend while taking advantage of the weakening leaders.

Buy shares or options on a lagging stock that's gaining both momentum and relative performance and sell XLB fund shares. Consider purchasing a seven-week call with a $12.50 strike (when the stock is at $12.36) for $1.05 on MWV, our current laggard. The break-even point is when MWV trades at $13.55 (strike plus premium), or 9.6 percent above the current stock price. At the same time, sell between 10 and 20 percent of your XLB position.

This strategy can also work on a broader scale. Many managers follow SPX and use it as a benchmark. SPY shares and options can let us mimic SPX's performance. SPX and its "child" SPY usually have a correlation of nearly 100 percent, so using it as a proxy for SPX—if that is our market benchmark—makes perfect sense. SPY also offers added

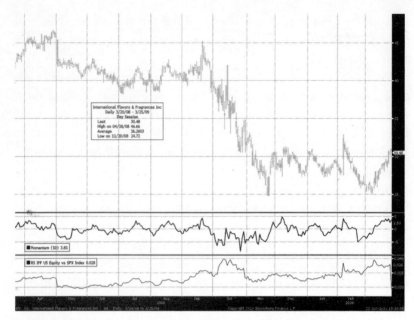

Figure 8.3 Daily chart for International Flavors & Fragences Inc.

liquidity, competitive pricing, and the ability to finely tune the strategy within a managed portfolio.

Exchange-traded funds provide new and more dynamic opportunities for strategy creation than do their larger parents. Sector funds can help managers hedge or speculate on a particular sector and in some cases an industry group, and they offer opportunities to use pair strategies.

CHAPTER 9

Efficient Pricing—Mostly

THE OPTIONS MARKETPLACE IS A largely efficient place, thanks to computerized trading across multiple exchanges, as well as to a group of traders called market makers, who commit to maintaining market liquidity by taking the opposing sides of trades when no other buyer or seller is available. But the options market is not always perfectly efficient. Small inefficiencies can offer profitable opportunities and suggest trading strategies.

Exploiting Small Pricing Inefficiencies

Theoretical values and models affect options contract pricing, but only to a degree. Like any free market product, options contracts are subject to the laws of supply and demand, which override all other pricing rules. Events and conditions may help create pricing that differs from the pricing models.

The forces of supply and demand work best when the markets contain enough liquidity for buyers and sellers to find each other. Market makers ensure that this is the case. Market makers work to make money for themselves, of course, but also commit to taking a reasonable number of contracts from the opposing side of a customer's trade. They may also purchase or sell shares in the underlying security in the process of adjusting their marketplace exposure, which offers important liquidity to both the options and equities markets.

The value of puts, calls, and the underlying stock price are all linked, so a change in one value affects the other two. (That's what we mean when we say that options are a derivative instrument.) As opportunities to capture arbitrage develop, professional options traders constantly monitor prices and move to take advantage of these openings.

To do this, traders often combine a call and put, with the same expiration and strike price, to synthetically create a long or short stock position. By putting these positions against the opposing underlying share position, traders virtually create neutral risk exposure. A long call paired with a short put has virtually the same risk/reward profile as a long stock position, and is known as a synthetic long position. A short call plus a long put position is equivalent to a short stock position, and is known as a synthetic short position.

Figure 9.1 illustrates a synthetic long position's potential movement and risk/reward profiles. The thick solid line (line S), which moves diagonally, represents the underlying stock price, or long stock position; line L shows the synthetic long position. Line C, the solid thinner line marked with a triangle, shows the call option; line P, the thinner line marked with a dot, represents the short put option. Line L is marked with a square, is actually a combination of lines C and P. Note that lines S and L have nearly identical movements, causing them to overlap.

Figure 9.2 is Figure 9.1's opposite, comparing the synthetic short position to the stock's normal short position. The thick solid line (line S) represents the short stock position. Line C, a thinner line marked with a triangle, represents a short call position; line P is a thin line marked with a dot and shows a long put contract. Line L, which is dotted, combines lines C and P. Once again, line L is nearly identical to line S.

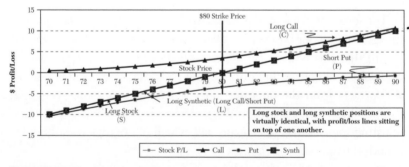

Figure 9.1 Graphic comparison of long stock position to a long call, short put, and long synthetic strategies.

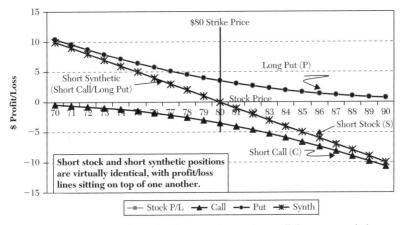

Figure 9.2 Graphic comparison of a short stock to a short call, long put, and short synthetic strategies.

In each of these charts, the synthetic positions are nearly identical to the real positions—but not exactly the same. The reason illustrates the differences between stock pricing and option pricing. Interest rates and dividend payments may in fact impact stock price, but in a less precise fashion than they impact option pricing. In general, rising interest rates push call values up and put values down. An increased dividend typically means higher put values and lower call prices.

Together, interest rates and dividends are known as the "cost of carry" (Figure 9.3).

To determine cost of carry for a long position, we subtract, or offset, dividends from interest rate. To find the carry cost of a short position, subtract interest rate from dividends. These cost-of-carry values are the difference between the synthetic positions and the similar natural positions. (Additionally, synthetic position holders are not entitled to vote at annual shareholder or special meetings.)

If the price of a particular call or put option rises or falls for any reason and the underlying security's price does not change, an opportunity to take advantage of the option's price change will develop. By creating a synthetic long or synthetic short position while simultaneously taking the opposing cash equity position, a trader can capture that difference with little risk until expiration.

This move is very similar to arbitrage strategies in which a trader buys stock on one exchange and sells it on another at a slightly higher price.

Strike Price	2/18/2010	2/20/2010	3/26/2010	4/17/2010	5/22/2010	6/19/2010	7/17/2010	8/21/2010	9/18/2010	10/16/2010	11/20/2010	12/18/2010	1/22/2011
5.0	1.01	1.03	1.05	1.07	1.09	1.11	1.13	1.15	1.17	1.19	1.22	1.24
7.5	1.01	1.04	1.07	1.11	1.13	1.16	1.20	1.23	1.26	1.29	1.32	1.36
10.0	1.01	1.05	1.09	1.14	1.18	1.22	1.27	1.31	1.34	1.39	1.43	1.48
12.5	1.02	1.07	1.11	1.18	1.22	1.27	1.33	1.38	1.43	1.49	1.54	1.60
15.0	1.02	1.08	1.14	1.21	1.27	1.33	1.40	1.46	1.52	1.59	1.65	1.72
17.5	1.02	1.09	1.16	1.25	1.31	1.38	1.47	1.53	1.60	1.68	1.76	1.84
20.0	1.03	1.11	1.18	1.28	1.36	1.44	1.53	1.61	1.69	1.79	1.86	1.96
22.5	1.03	1.12	1.21	1.32	1.40	1.49	1.60	1.69	1.71	1.88	1.97	1.88
25.0	1.03	1.13	1.23	1.35	1.45	1.55	1.67	1.76	1.86	1.98	1.88	1.28
27.5	1.04	1.15	1.25	1.39	1.49	1.60	1.73	1.84	1.95	1.98	1.19	1.32
30.0	1.04	1.16	1.28	1.42	1.54	1.65	1.80	1.92	1.03	1.18	1.33	1.44
32.5	1.05	1.17	1.30	1.46	1.58	1.71	1.87	1.99	1.12	1.20	1.48	1.56
35.0	1.05	1.18	1.32	1.49	1.63	1.76	1.93	1.07	1.21	1.30	1.51	1.68
37.5	1.05	1.20	1.34	1.53	1.67	1.82	1.00	1.15	1.29	1.40	1.62	1.80
40.0	1.06	1.21	1.37	1.56	1.72	1.87	1.07	1.22	1.38	1.57	1.73	1.92
42.5	1.06	1.22	1.39	1.60	1.76	1.93	1.13	1.30	1.46	1.67	1.84	2.04
45.0	1.06	1.24	1.41	1.63	1.81	1.98	1.20	1.38	1.55	1.77	1.94	2.16
47.5	1.07	1.25	1.44	1.67	1.85	1.04	1.27	1.45	1.64	1.87	2.05	2.28
50.0	1.07	1.26	1.46	1.71	1.90	1.09	1.33	1.53	1.72	1.97	2.16	2.40
55.0	1.08	1.29	1.50	1.77	1.99	1.20	1.47	1.68	1.89	2.16	2.38	2.64
60.0	1.08	1.32	1.55	1.84	1.88	1.31	1.60	1.83	2.07	2.36	2.59	2.88
65.0	1.09	1.34	1.60	1.91	1.16	1.42	1.73	1.99	2.24	2.55	2.81	3.12
70.0	1.10	1.37	1.64	1.98	1.25	1.53	1.87	2.14	2.41	2.75	3.02	3.36
75.0	1.10	1.40	1.69	2.05	1.34	1.64	2.00	2.29	2.58	2.95	3.24	3.60
80.0	1.11	1.42	1.73	2.12	1.43	1.74	2.13	2.44	2.76	3.14	3.46	3.84
85.0	1.12	1.45	1.78	2.19	1.52	1.85	2.27	2.60	2.93	3.34	3.67	4.08
90.0	1.13	1.48	1.83	2.26	1.61	1.96	2.40	2.75	3.10	3.54	3.89	4.32
95.0	1.13	1.50	1.87	2.33	1.70	2.07	2.53	2.90	3.27	3.73	4.10	4.57
300.0	1.14	1.53	1.92	2.40	1.79	2.18	2.67	3.06	3.44	3.93	4.32	4.81
305.0	1.15	1.55	1.96	2.47	1.88	2.29	2.80	3.21	3.62	4.13	4.54	5.05
310.0	1.15	1.58	1.81	1.54	1.97	2.40	2.93	3.36	3.79	4.32	4.75	5.29
315.0	1.16	1.61	1.85	1.61	2.06	2.51	3.07	3.51	3.96	4.52	4.97	5.53
320.0	1.17	1.63	1.10	2.15	2.62	3.20	3.67	4.13	4.72	5.18	5.77
325.0	1.17	1.66	1.15	1.75	2.24	2.73	3.33	3.82	4.31	4.91	5.40	6.01
330.0	1.18	1.69	1.19	1.82	2.33	2.83	3.47	3.97	4.48	5.11	5.62	6.25
335.0	1.19	1.71	1.24	1.89	2.42	2.94	3.60	4.13	4.65	5.31	5.83	6.49
340.0	1.19	1.74	1.28	1.96	2.51	3.05	3.73	4.28	4.82	5.50	6.05	6.73
345.0	1.20	1.77	1.33	2.03	2.60	3.16	3.87	4.43	4.99	5.70	6.26	6.97
350.0	1.21	1.79	1.38	2.10	2.69	3.27	4.00	4.58	5.17	5.90	6.48	7.21
355.0	1.22	1.82	1.42	2.17	2.78	3.38	4.13	4.74	5.34	6.10	6.71	7.45
360.0	1.22	1.84	1.47	2.24	2.87	3.49	4.27	4.89	5.51	6.29	6.91	7.69

Figure 9.3 Cost of carry.

Before computerized pricing efficiencies, pricing time lags could mean that a stock cost less on one exchange than traders bid for it on another, allowing traders to capture the price difference by attempting to execute simultaneous buy and sell orders.

In the options world, purchasing shares and implementing a synthetic short position is known as a forward conversion, or a conversion strategy. Sell shares short and build a synthetic long position, and you have a reverse conversion, or a reversal strategy. These strategies carry little to no risk, except for potential changes in interest rates and dividend payments. The positions virtually offset each other, so traders know that shares will either be sold (a conversion) or repurchased (a reversal) at the strike price, regardless of how high or low the security price goes. An investor will exercise the long option, and the short option will likely be assigned if either is in the money at expiration. If an option's long holder doesn't exercise the position, under the rules of the Options Clearing Corp. (OCC) the arbitrageur benefits further by closing the stock position at a more favorable price.

There is the risk, however, of premature assignment. If an option's short portion is assigned before expiration and just before a dividend ex-date, the holder may miss out on pocketing the dividend as part of his or her position.

Special dividends, splits, and other corporate payments or adjustments may also hold risks. Sometimes these risks are evident in option prices, which may seem out of sync with other, comparable derivatives. For example, a stock dividend that is based on a percentage of the underlying share price, or an unknown dividend payment—from a foreign security, for instance—may result in a greater variety of option prices, or in options prices that seem completely out of line with their theoretical values or arbitrage situations. This might be due to a currency conversion or other element that can affect the pricing of the underlying security or options.

Let's take a look at a normal situation, compare options to the underlying stock, and show how arbitrage situations help keep options prices in line with underlying stock value. A stock with relatively high pricing and volatility will aid our illustration.

On July 2, a share of First Solar Corp. (FSLR), which did not pay a dividend, cost $154.20. Calls with an August expiration and a $155 strike price (commonly referred to as August 155 calls) were $13.40 bid to $13.90 offered, and the August 155 puts were $14.30 bid to $14.50 offered. Implied volatility was 59.62 percent. We'll compare two resulting scenarios.

Scenario #1—Long Stock Synthetic Short (Forward Conversion)
+100 shares FSLR at $154.20
– 1 Aug 155 Call at $13.60 (split bid and offer)
+ 1 Aug 155 Put at $14.40 (split bid and offer)
Net debit is $155.00.

The combination of a short call and long put position resemble a short stock position, offsetting the long stock position's risk. The net debit of $155 is also the total purchase price. The strike price of both put and call are also $155, so we break even by selling the position at $155 (excluding cost of carry). Consider cost of carry, and the trade carries a loss of $0.89 per share, based on an interest rate of 5 percent and approximately six weeks to expiration.

Execute the options at the most favorable prices, buying the call at $13.40 (the bid) and selling the put at $14.50 (the offer), and the added 30 cents per share give a net debit of $154.70. Even in the best (and nearly impossible) scenario, a trader would still lose $0.59 per share.

If a combination of declining call and rising put bumped the spread above a loss of $0.89 per share, traders would move in, knowing that they could make a few cents per share at virtually zero risk.

If the stock price suddenly moved lower by more than 30 cents and the corresponding options only adjusted by 25 cents, a trader might earn five cents per share.

Scenario #2—Short Stock Synthetic Long (Reverse Conversion)
−100 Shares FSLR at $154.20
+ 1 Aug 155 Call at $13.60 (split bid and offer)
−1 Aug 155 Put at $14.40 (split bid and offer)
Net credit is $155.

In this scenario the long call and short put position create a synthetic long stock position, offsetting the risk of the short stock position. The net credit of $155 is also the total position's selling price. The strike price of put plus call is $155, which is also the purchase price. Excluding cost of carry, the trade breaks even. Including cost of carry, the trade yields a profit of $0.27 per share, based on an interest rate of 1.5 percent over approximately six weeks.

The split between bid and offer prices offers a $0.27 per-share profit with virtually no risk, but it may be difficult to actually execute at those prices. The risk-free profit, however, may still be worth pursuing, particularly if an investor can execute the trade in large share lots of perhaps 10,000 or more.

If the prices move, these scenarios may change. By initiating an original long stock position at $154.25 and locking in a sale at $155, traders could net a profit of $0.75 per share, as long as they paid no interest on borrowed capital. Sell the original shares at $155.80 and repurchase them at $155, conversely, and you'll take a profit of $0.80 a share, excluding interest earned. This would be an attractive trade.

Market maker traders often pursue these types of trades, appreciating their lack of risk and locked-in profits. The per-share profits are small, but they can rapidly add up. It's a bit like owning a newsstand. You make a small profit on each lottery ticket or candy bar; sell enough of them, and you enjoy a nice income.

Market makers, specialists, upstairs traders, and others often have customized computer programs that scan for these opportunities.

Traders benefit from these trades' low risk and generally locked-in profits. Furthermore, this type of arbitrage can help them produce steady income while also leaving them open to other, more lucrative (and riskier) strategies.

Another example shows similar results. Using a simpler, mega-cap stock such as 3M Corp. (MMM), we can show options pricing efficiency for lower-volatility stocks. MMM has an implied volatility of 27.74 percent and a last sale price of $60.25. In the near-month July options, $60 strike calls are priced between $1.25 and $1.35; comparable puts are $1.00 to $1.10. (Spreads here, on a stock with lower pricing and volatility, are narrower than in our previous example.)

To create a long conversion, purchase the shares, then sell the call while purchasing the put, for a net debit of $60.10. (There is no dividend during the holding period.) The interest cost (5 percent annual interest on $60.25 for two weeks) would be $0.116 per share. Therefore, the strategy would result in a loss of 21.6 cents per share—not a good goal, as the trader has committed to selling the stock at $60 per share.

Again using correct bid and offer prices, a reversal would give a net credit of $59.90 per share. Adding an interest credit of $0.035 per share (1.5 percent annual interest on $60.25 for two weeks) narrows the anticipated loss to 6.5 cents per share—not as bad, but still a loss.

The call strategy becomes more favorable if the option's call price increases or the put value decreases. A movement of about a quarter point for either option, a combination of both that equals a quarter point, or a lower stock price and downward options adjustments of at least $0.25 would all make the strategy feasible. The trade could be profitable with a net debit of $59.85 or lower.

The reversal could also be profitable if a change in the underlying stock price yielded a net credit of $59.97 or more.

Other factors can also affect pricing, particularly in reversals. These variables include rebates for borrowed stock, the ability to borrow stock, volatility changes, changing interest rates, rumors and stories, dividends, and general market activity. Note, too, that cost-of-carry values may include transaction and clearing costs, which may increase or decrease and thereby create narrower profits, turn profits into losses, or mean a different break-even point.

Consider this generic example. Two-month puts and calls on a stock trading at $25.07 with a strike price of $25 and a volatility reading of 21.97 percent both have thetas of −0.0075. The theoretical value of both the put and the call will decline by approximately one cent (rounded up) per day for the next several days, if none of the other variables change. (Thetas always change daily, because the number of days to expiration is one of the input variables.)

CHAPTER 10

The Subprime Mortgage Crisis and Options

THE OPTIONS MARKET is generally efficient—but there are times when the market gets out of sorts, in ways both anticipated and surprising. One of these instances involved a relatively new event that changed trading for several weeks during the autumn of 2008, one that many traders and investors never envisioned. Though the event lasted for weeks, the potential impact lingers on.

The worldwide equities market was melting down. Lehman Brothers (LEH) became insolvent, following American International Group's (AIG) government bailout. This led to a near-total collapse of the equities markets, especially in the financial sector. Counterparty risk on over-the-counter and even exchange-traded stocks, options, and other instruments came under scrutiny, and volatility was at one of its highest points ever.

Regulators looked at every possible way to stabilize the markets. One idea was to eliminate short sales of stocks in or closely tied to the financial sector, a group that included banks, brokers, and insurance companies. Even firms such as General Electric and General Motors, both of whom had financial operations, were in the mix when regulators implemented this measure.

The cash equities and options markets were unnerved. Options traders couldn't sell stock short, so they couldn't purchase calls and sell puts to offset positions. That further damaged the cash and derivatives marketplace. Spreads widened sharply, liquidity tanked, and implied volatility levels rose to all-time highs. The CBOE S&P 500 Implied Volatility Index (VIX) reading topped 90 percent for the first time, effectively shutting down the markets, as market makers and other traders could not manage risk. This ultimately forced the whole market further south.

During the 1987 market crash and 1989's mini-crash, traders attempted to shield themselves from growing risk. Some market makers walked out of crowds; others took on limited positions. Others were assigned trades through automated systems and tried to reduce their risk exposure after learning of their new positions.

Some people thought market makers needed to step up and assume risk, regardless of the trading situation. Market makers' own risk managers, bosses, and bankers, however, warned of the potential long-term consequences of doing so: reduced positions, firm closures, circuit breakers, and potential market shutdowns. Problems during fall 2008 were expected to be short-term, so many traders just kept positions small.

Managing Delta

Professional traders may also employ other strategies that limit risk while providing liquidity. One popular risk technique is called *delta neutral*. Similar to the arbitrage techniques discussed earlier, delta neutral strategies look to offset positions and risk, but not necessarily by 100 percent. Delta neutral strategies may or may not involve creating opposing synthetic positions. Delta neutral trading may begin with a synthetic position, or may grow to include such strategies.

A delta neutral position is based on the deltas of traded options. As mentioned before, the theoretical value of an option is based on an options pricing model, such as the Black-Scholes options pricing model, as well as on evolving market conditions. Such models produce the delta, also known as the hedge ratio, before they determine a theoretical value. A delta reading says how much a theoretical value should move over the short term (a few days), given a 1-point change in the underlying stock. At that point, the delta itself also changes. This change to the delta is known as the gamma, which is—for all intents and purposes—the delta's delta.

A stock has a delta of 100 percent. A long stock position has a +100 percent (or +1) delta; a short stock position has a –100 percent (or –1 delta), with the minus sign indicating the inverse relationship. Long calls and short puts have positive delta readings; short calls and long puts have negative delta readings.

Puts and calls with the same strike and expiration month, added together to form a synthetic long or synthetic short position, have a combined delta of +1 (synthetic long) or –1 (synthetic short). This is how traders combine options to offset the opposing stock position. Regardless of the stock's direction, the combination will always have a reading of plus or minus 1 or 100 percent.

Delta Relationships of Stocks and Options

We have discussed the protective put strategy, which traders use to hedge long stock positions against possible price deterioration. If the put is exercised, the holder can sell the stock at the put's strike price, allowing the holder to exit the position at a known risk level.

Position	Delta Reading
Long Stock	Positive
Short Stock	Negative
Long Call	Positive
Short Call	Negative
Long Put	Negative
Short Put	Positive

Consider another hypothetical example, this one with a twist: the delta twist. Stock XYZ is trading at $23.37. A six-week put with a $23 strike is trading between $1.06 (bid) to $1.09 (offer). The option's theoretical value is $0.92; the delta is –0.42. (Remember that the minus sign denotes the inverse relationship to the stock price.) By purchasing this put along with the stock, we hedge our position.

The delta reading of –0.42 means that, at the stock price's next 1-point, downward move—from $23.37 to $22.37—the put contract's theoretical value increases by $0.42 to $1.34. A gamma reading of 0.14 indicates that the delta will increase from –0.42 to –0.56. Conversely, if XYZ rose from $23.37 to $24.37, the put's theoretical value would drop from $0.92 to $0.50. The delta would also likely decline from –0.42 to –0.28.

Now look at a covered call on XYZ. A six-week call with a $25 strike is trading with a bid-offer market of $0.52 to $0.55. This contract has a theoretical value of $0.51 and a delta of 0.31. This means that, if the stock rises from \$23.37 to \$24.37, the option's theoretical value increases to \$0.82, giving a net increase for the covered write position of \$0.69 per share (\$1.00 − \$0.31). A gamma of 0.13 tells us that the delta will rise from 0.31 to 0.44 on this movement as well, while the gamma drops from 0.13 to 0.12. A single-point stock price increase, from \$24.37 to \$25.37, should move the option's theoretical value from \$0.82 to \$1.26 and increase the delta from 0.44 to 0.56. The change moves this option into the money, though only by a few cents.

In-the-money options generally have a delta reading above 50 percent; out-of-the-money options typically have a delta reading below 50 percent. Options that are just barely in the money, with stock price and strike price virtually even, should have a reading (put or call) of 50 percent, though readings of 51 percent for the call and 49 percent for the put are also fairly common. (The inverse of these readings may also appear.)

Deltas may not add up to one for every options set. This may be partially due to the data vendor's rounding error or happen because a data source doesn't offer scores that add to 100 percent. Some vendors may use one model for call options and another for puts, which can throw off readings slightly. You'll find readings between 98 percent and 102 percent, none of which make the model invalid. For most traders, consistency is more important than a model's absolute accuracy. Professionals may be using several models, including a risk program, to determine their exposure and movements.

The deeper an option contract is in the money, the higher its delta reading. Conversely, the further an option is out of the money, the lower its delta. Therefore, a put and call in the same line will always have a 100 percent delta versus the stock, but their individual relationship will change. Figure 10.1 shows delta changing as stock price adjusts for both a put and call option.

Understanding deltas and their properties helps traders understand options and how they are priced and traded. That, in turn, helps any manager build and maintain options market positions while also managing risks. You don't need to become an expert and compute every single delta movement or theoretical value, but you do need to understand how options professionals trade contracts.

Market makers and options professionals use other trading methods that also deal with deltas. Married/protective puts, covered writes,

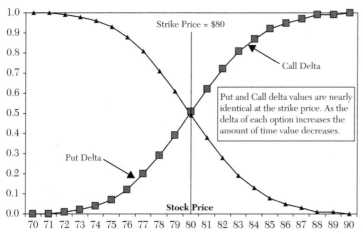

Figure 10.1 Comparison of the deltas of puts and calls, with the same expiration date and same strike price. Note the inverse relationship and movement of these values as the price of the stock rises and falls.

options arbitrage, and some other strategies evaluate risk on a quantity basis, based on a relationship of 100 stock shares versus one call and/or one put.

Another type of hedging involves using deltas to neutralize positions. This type of position management requires constant adjusting—a usual part of the job for market makers and professional traders, but potentially a problem for fund managers. Understanding it, however, helps managers understand how the market works.

Let's begin with a simple example. Here are some puts and calls for the next two (hypothetical) months:

		Stock Price = $24.64		
Call Price	**Delta**	**Month/Strike**	**Put Price**	**Delta**
4.65	1.00	1Mon/20	0.00	0.00
3.70	0.99	1Mon/21	0.00	−0.01
2.65	0.97	1Mon/22	0.02	−0.03
1.74	0.87	1Mon/23	0.11	−0.13
0.99	0.68	1Mon/24	0.34	−0.32
0.48	0.43	1Mon/25	0.80	−0.57

(*continued*)

		Stock Price = $24.64		
Call Price	**Delta**	**Month/Strike**	**Put Price**	**Delta**
0.18	0.21	1Mon/26	1.51	−0.79
0.06	0.08	1Mon/27	2.39	−0.92
0.01	0.02	1Mon/28	3.33	−0.98
0.00	0.00	1Mon/29	4.33	−1.00
4.75	0.95	2Mon/20	0.06	−0.05
3.83	0.91	2Mon/21	0.15	−0.09
2.97	0.83	2Mon/22	0.31	−0.17
2.24	0.73	2Mon/23	0.58	−0.28
1.60	0.61	2Mon/24	0.96	−0.39
1.11	0.48	2Mon/25	1.47	−0.52
0.74	0.36	2Mon/26	2.10	−0.64
0.47	0.26	2Mon/27	2.83	−0.74
0.29	0.18	2Mon/28	3.63	−0.82
0.17	0.12	2Mon/29	4.51	−0.88

We can create various scenarios with virtually neutral deltas without much effort. Here are some examples:

extremely crucial

1. Ratio Bull Spread: Long 1 2-Month Call with a 23 Strike and Short 2 2-Month Calls with a 26 Strike—Deltas are +0.73 − (2 × −0.36) = + 0.01 deltas

2. Butterfly Spread: Long 1 2-Month Call with a 24 Strike, Short 2 2-Month Calls with a 26 Strike, Long 1 2-Month Call with a 28 Strike—Deltas are +0.61 − (2 X −0.72) + 0.18 = +0.07 deltas.

3. Collar: Long 100 shares of stock, Short 1 Month Call with a 25 Strike, long 1 Month Put with a 24 Strike—Deltas are +100 − 0.43 + −0.32 = + 25 deltas

As you see, we can mix and match to adjust our long or short exposure for a 1-point stock movement. For example, in our third potential strategy, deltas are not completely neutral—they are + 25, meaning that the position should theoretically rise 25 cents for each 1-point increase in the underlying stock and decrease 25 cents for each 1-point stock decrease. When the combined delta figure is negative, gains and losses are inverse to the stock's movements.

Traders may use these position adjustments to control risk. They may also go further by looking at gamma neutral positioning, which provides additional hedging against price movement. Gamma neutral positioning details are beyond the scope of this book.

When traders use delta and gamma hedges, they leave room to adjust for risk, especially when a stock is volatile or gaps higher or lower at the opening bell or after a stopped trade. Traders may make small incremental position changes or introduce other options contracts to adjust positions as trading conditions warrant. Traders know that their positions may become completely out of sync on these occasions, rendering their strategies worthless and subjecting them to increased risk.

Deltas may also be used to adjust positions comprised of odd-lot stock quantities. Perhaps a fund owns 674 shares of a stock. The trader may create a delta neutral strategy by selling eight in-the-money calls with a delta of 0.84, yielding an offsetting position of 672 deltas to the 674 long deltas, or a net long of two deltas.

Delta hedging strategies aren't always the best way to protect a position, but they can provide opportunities to make money: the primary reason traders use them. Their partial hedge value helps protect the trader from completely naked exposure. For this, the trader usually gives up some return.

Completely hedged positions, such as the arbitrage examples illustrated earlier, generally permit only minimal gains. This is where the balance of risk and reward comes into play. The safer the positions, the less money an investor can make. Riskier positions mean higher potential gains, but also a higher potential for losses. Experienced traders understand this and take risks in some positions while reducing risks in others. They adjust hedges to meet changing markets, sectors, industry groups, and even individual stocks.

Traders also look at many other market factors. Unlike fund managers, traders constantly monitor intraday charts that track changes over one, five, or 60 minutes, as well as tick charts, which offer data that's based on each occurring trade, not time. Traders follow news, sudden market movements, volatility changes, and movement size. They watch standard deviations to help them control risk and to find opportunities in short-term trend reversals.

Fund managers may not have the time or inclination to use all these tools. For them, Bollinger Bands can help monitor daily chart movement on a daily chart, showing some extremes on a time scale that is more in line with an investment scenario. Bollinger Bands are normally placed two standard deviations both above and below a stock's 20-day moving average, allowing investment managers to see short-term movements without monitoring nearly every tick. Those standard deviations are also a method of monitoring volatility.

CHAPTER 11

The Other Greeks

DELTAS AND GAMMAS ARE NOT the only pricing data that concern market markers. Several other factors help these traders maintain their positions and adjust for changing risk exposures.

Theta shows the expected change, also called *deterioration*, in a single option premium over time, typically 24 hours. Because time-based premium decay tends to accelerate toward a contract's expiration, the theta is expected to increase as expiration nears. (See Figures 11.1 and 11.2.) By understanding the relationship among time, expiration, and premiums, traders can adjust positions—especially those in the current expiration month—so as to avoid substantial, time-linked losses. I often monitor theta over three-day holiday weekends. For example, a call option based on a stock trading at $31.36 has 36 calendar days before the next expiration, a strike price of $31, and a volatility of 43.34 percent. The contract's theoretical value is $1.83 and its theta is –0.0241. The theoretical value is expected to decline by about 2 1/2 cents over the next day, if there are no other variable changes. Using that information, we can conclude that the value of that contract will likely erode by about 7 1/2 cents over a three-day weekend. This can change a manager's decision about when to buy or sell that contract.

Understanding theta can be very useful to managers in various situations. Perhaps you hold a position in puts or calls and want to know how the value of that position may change if the stock remains near its current price during the Christmas holiday week. Or you might wonder whether you should purchase an option two weeks before an event, or how long you should wait before making that purchase, in cases where

115

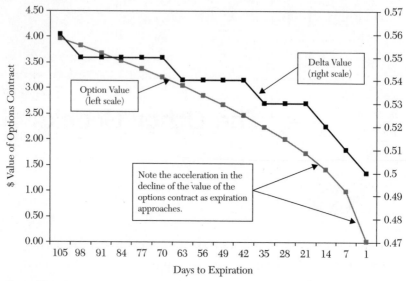

Figure 11.1 This chart illustrates the time value erosion of an at-the-money option (put or call) during a period of nearly three months. Notice how the angle of descent changes as the option enters its final month of life.

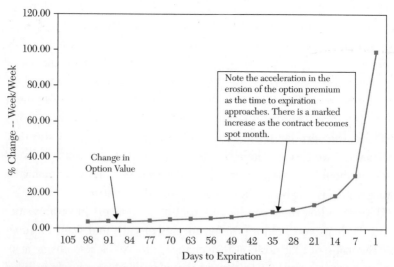

Figure 11.2 This chart shows the incremental week/week loss in value as the time premium of the option decays. Note the sharp upward move as a greater percentage of the option evaporates on a weekly basis.

day-to-day changes will have little impact on the portfolio. The relationship between time and price may be very important or have little significance. Theta will determine which is true for you.

Vega shows the relationship between a volatility change and an option premium, which typically change together. Interestingly, volatility's relationship to both calls and puts is virtually the same. As volatility increases, so do premiums for both puts and calls, though at different levels for each option contract. Traders apply vega to individual contracts, not to the underlying security.

Interest rate changes affect a stock's cost of carry, and thus impact options value now and potentially in the future. Rho shows the change in option value based on a change in interest rates. Rising rates normally lift call premiums and reduce put premiums. Conversely, falling interest rates depress call values and increase put premiums. Several vendors do not provide rho information.

Market makers may refer to these valuations frequently or infrequently, depending on the type of trading that they are doing and the risk controls in place. Most firms associated with these traders provide a daily sheet (some more frequently) that shows their positions, as well as many of the risk valuations we've reviewed. This information may also be available via computer. Wireless hand-held terminals have become popular for this type of trading and risk control.

Other Products

Along with the Chicago Board Options Exchange (CBOE), I helped introduce equity flex options, which are designed for institutional managers' needs. These options let managers customize exchange-traded contracts, allowing them to achieve configurations that they normally could only get by using over-the-counter options.

An equity flex option lets users customize the exercise price, the contract's date of expiration (out to five years, but not within three days of normal expiration), and the option settlement style, which can be American— an option may be exercised/assigned on any day before expiration—or European style, in which an option may only be exercised or assigned on the last day of its life. American-style options usually have slightly higher premiums than their European-style equivalents. Tailored strike prices are also available; these allow the user to truly customize the contract.

Ex-Dividend Trades

Watch option volumes and activity jump, and you'll typically find stocks that will trade ex-dividend.

Dividend capture strategies normally occur just prior to the ex-dividend date. Traders look to purchase inexpensive option contracts, exercise those contracts to collect the dividend, and then sell the underlying shares. Traders often buy these contracts within the spot expiration month, with little or no time premium, or at a discount to their intrinsic value. A discount may occur when the option's price is below its true economic value, meaning that the cost of owning the stock, if the call were exercised immediately, would be less than the stock's current price. This usually occurs for options that are in the money and have no time premium remaining.

Traders have also been known to use spreads: buying one call and selling the other. They plan to exercise the long call and hope that the short call will not be exercised before the ex-dividend date. If the short option is exercised ahead of the dividend and before the trader exercises the long call, the stock would change hands before becoming ex-dividend, yielding a flat position with no dividend capture. Exercise the long call when the short call is left alone, by contrast, and a trader captures the dividend and holds a covered write position. Spreads let traders use the short option contract premium to either offset the long contract time premium or the option's purchase price.

Market makers also employ strategies before anticipated events. Some of these trades may be against an existing position, either in stock or other options; others may stand alone. Traders may use volatility trades, such as buying straddles or strangles, before an expected earnings announcement, for instance.

A straddle involves purchasing or selling put and call options with the same expiration and striking prices. Strangles involve selling or purchasing put and call options with the same expiration date, but strike prices that are above (for the call) and below (for the put) the security's current price. Straddles and strangles strategies let traders participate in strong movements regardless of direction, but they are normally used only when implied volatility levels are low. High premiums mean that traders need larger market movements to reach a break-even point, making the strategy less effective.

Getting Information from the Exchange Floor

Though many aspects of trading have turned electronic, professional options traders still have invaluable information. They often know more about a security's movements, as they follow those movements all day long. Their positions and subsequent risks may also mean that they collect information from back office support staff and other traders. This information may be public, but still not widely known.

I remember feeling intrigued that options on Honda Motor (HMC) were trading between $0.75 and $1.50—an unlikely price during a reversing market. This was a great opportunity to lock in a significant profit for the next 45 days or so, but no one was trading it. I checked with my back office, called an analyst, and even contacted the floor on the New York Stock Exchange to speak with the stock specialist. Nothing.

Then I checked with my floor broker on the Philadelphia Stock Exchange, where the options were trading. The traders explained that the HMC board of directors was expected to declare an increased dividend within a few days, and that increased volatility in the U.S. dollar's relationship to the Japanese yen had made it nearly impossible to accurately calculate the value of the options contract.

At another time I looked at options on a biotechnology company that was rumored to be a potential acquisition target. It seemed that some of the options were out of line with the market—especially in the put contracts, which were trading well above anticipated levels. I contacted my associates on the floor of the Chicago Board Options Exchange (CBOE) to get more information. It's possible for put options to trade higher when some traders think there will be no takeover, or reject the idea that the stock price will drop if a takeover does occur. In reality, I found that other rumors suggested that the Food and Drug Administration would hold up the company's potential drug approval. This overshadowed any potential acquisition in many professionals' minds, because it could change the company's earnings projections—and therefore its value. Negative news from clinical trials could also affect other drugs that were already on the market, potentially resulting in a drop in sales, potential accounting write-offs, or even lawsuits from patients already taking the drug. No wonder the puts were priced so high.

CHAPTER 12

When Conditions Change

MARKETS ARE ALWAYS CHANGING, affected by everything from seasonality to labor laws. Change is normal, and exchange-traded markets and securities are no exception to this rule.

There are times, however, when changes push the limits of what's "normal" for markets, changing marketplace dynamics. Both routine and extreme changes can change portfolio management strategies.

Routine Changes

To see how routine changes affect portfolios, imagine a managed fund that concentrates on purchasing large-cap securities and writing calls against those shares. The fund's primary goal is to earn a return that exceeds the S&P 500 Index (SPX) performance by at least 2 percent. Fund guidelines say that an option premium must be at least 4 percent of the underlying stock price, with a minimum of 2 1/2 percent upside potential between the security's current price and the written call's strike price.

Seasonal and other market factors will make this strategy easy to implement at certain times of the year and hard at other points. Assume that today is August 1 and that International Business Machines (IBM) is trading at $117.93. The stock has appreciated 40.1 percent so far this year. (IBM normally doesn't rise that strongly; it has an average annual appreciation rate of approximately 9 percent over the prior 20 years.)

The broad market has been strong. Options expiring over the next 30-day period (average between August and September) have a risk reading of 22.97 percent, based on the implied volatility of the at-the-money options. The 60-day implied volatility reading is 25.95 percent, nearly 13 percent higher than the same figure during the current period. Figure 12.1 shows the implied volatility skew for IBM at-the-money contracts.

Both the broad market and IBM shares appreciated dramatically during this period, likely driving the sharp premium increase. In combination with the seasonally weak September–October period, all these factors indicate that traders expect additional volatility—in this case, over the next six months.

By contrast, current risk is very low, particularly compared to this chart's "normal" readings, so traders who write calls against the stock will earn below-normal premiums. As a result, the fund manager will find it difficult to use a call-writing strategy and still stay within fund guidelines.

As in this example, a stock, sector, or market can move out of "normal" range to the low end as well as to the high end. Lower readings might follow earnings reports or other factors, some of them unique to an individual stock, industry group, or sector.

Of course, abnormally high readings are also a possibility. These may follow periods of rising interest rates, which may in turn increase volatility

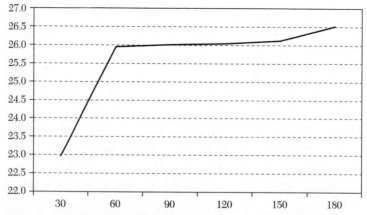

Figure 12.1 Implied volatility skew on International Business Machines (IBM).

for stocks that feel the pain of higher borrowing costs: utilities, large industrial manufacturers, and others. Trading patterns and volatility levels may change after the Fed increases interest rates, for instance, or after a sharp decline in the bond market.

The Extremes

Other periods seem to defy the rules. In a bell curve based on a 95 percent confidence interval (Figure 12.2), data points will lie between point A and point B at least 95 percent of the time. More extreme movements occur in the 2-1/2 percent on either side, though of course some outliers may range beyond the bell's scope. The sharpest movements may be between three and five times greater, or even more, than those in the normal range.

Single events and larger, more comprehensive changes may create severe market movements. Severe, unpredicted movements can quickly change entire markets and may also force adjustments to analytical methods.

On March 30, 1981, President Ronald Reagan was the target of a would-be assassin. The shooting happened outside the entrance to the Washington Hilton, where gunman Mark Hinckley fired six shots, hitting the president three times. News of the attack quickly hit news services and the market turned negative nearly instantaneously before

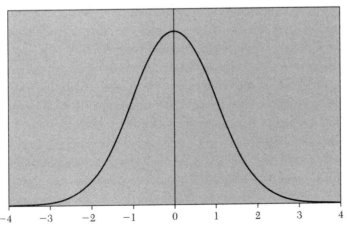

Figure 12.2 Normalized bell curve with 95% confidence interval.

officials shut down trading. Prices were not reliable and market makers could not commit to large trades.

In October 1987 the stock market crashed, offering up the worst performance in decades, with the Dow Jones Industrial Average (DJIA) recording its largest single-session decline of 508 points.

Put buyers attempted to buy contracts; call writers tried to sell. Markets were points apart compared to normal trading periods, and premiums jumped off the scale. Options that were 25 points out of the money had quotes of $40 per share or more. Implied volatility levels were well off the charts and pricing models stopped working. The market became extremely emotional and completely irrational.

Computerized trading was ramping up at the time. Program trades, which let traders enter orders on baskets of stocks, couldn't keep up with the price changes, which in turn couldn't keep up with changes in the pits. Many firms turned off computerized trading services, because executed prices did not come close to the values traders anticipated when they entered their orders.

Volume can also affect prices and models during periods of severe movements. Order size and number often increase during unstable periods, which adds to the problems. Market imbalances cause difficulties. Uncertain markets mean more transmitted data, with additional opportunities for mistakes. The electronic systems that pair buyers and sellers don't work well. One-sided pressure, usually downward, results in more imbalances.

When data are unreliable, the systems that link stock data to their corresponding options can also break down. Out-of-sequence prints, bad quotes, and other factors may disengage volatility models from reality.

When these models become unreliable, it's best to use simple strategies and move slowly. Adjusting out of positions can be difficult. Bad pricing and volatility data can yield poor position valuations with inflated or undervalued gains and losses. Limit orders are a great idea for price-sensitive managers—but remember that there is no guarantee that an order will be filled.

Look at intrinsic values and positions, pairing long and short exposure and attempting to net positions as if each option were at expiration. Review your naked exposure (long or short), then adjust your risk.

Next, compare current and intrinsic valuations to try to see your exposure, as well as how much the pricing models differ. If you are short an out-of-the-money option with a $25 per share time premium, that might indicate potential, but not immediate risk. Likewise, determining exposure by comparing intrinsic and current market values is a good situational strategy for in-the-money options.

Many brokerage firms use margin requirements that are above industry minimums. Rules permit them to change these requirements as risk levels change—so they may raise margin requirements now. The exchanges, the Options Clearing Corp., the Securities and Exchange Commission (SEC), and the Treasury also are allowed to change margin requirements and maintenance rules, especially during periods of higher volatility and market risk. This may result in higher capital demands and/or position closings.

During the 1987 market crash some firms eliminated traders' ability to sell naked options, some targeted index options, and some raised margin requirements significantly. This, once again, affected the markets by changing both supply and demand dynamics and liquidity. Bid/offer spreads widened as many companies refused to initiate new opening positions. Some also increased margin interest levels, meaning higher borrowing costs for both investors and market makers.

Sudden market extremes can affect your portfolio holdings and risk levels—but the extremes (and the volatility and risk levels they create) don't usually last very long.

Meet the New Rules

Some new rules and regulations are long-term changes; others are meant for certain shorter-term situations. For example, in 2001 the options exchanges began phasing in new pricing requirements that reflect stock trading; the new rules narrow the bid-offer spreads by requiring quotes in pennies instead of fractions. This is a long-term change that regulators hope will lead to a more competitive marketplace.

Other changes are based on unusual market conditions. The worst market conditions of the 2007–2009 credit crisis occurred in the fourth quarter of 2008. The CBOE S&P 500 Implied Volatility Index (VIX) rose to an all-time high of 89.53 percent (Figure 12.3), just as the market nearly shut down. From cash equities to options, traders were not able to make markets. Investors were like deer on the road, stunned and blinded by truck headlights.

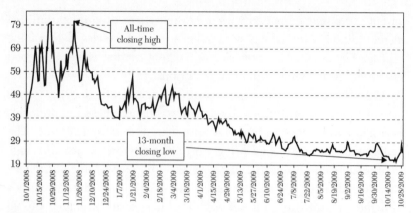

Figure 12.3 CBOE S&P 500 Implied Volatility Index (VIX)—Weekly chart from January 2006 to August 2009, showing the extreme jump in volatility readings during the 4Q of 2008.

The SEC enacted emergency rules that stopped *everyone* from short selling shares of financial and finance-related companies. This virtually shut down the options markets, as it meant that market makers couldn't provide liquidity by shorting stock to offset risk. Other sectors were also impacted. A squeeze on options market liquidity meant less liquidity in the equities market. Hedges were either unavailable or very expensive, so many portfolio managers couldn't hedge long or short positions.

Some market participants have called for eliminating the over-the-counter (OTC) market for derivatives due to their lack of liquidity, transparency, oversight, and regulation. These factors increase risk; according to some, they increase systemic risk. Such an action could provide further liquidity to the listed markets and their products.

Some options exchanges provide facilities for trading FLEX options contracts. Initiated by the Chicago Board Options Exchange (CBOE), FLEX options let institutional managers customize some option characteristics. They may be able to change the exercise/settlement feature from American style (can be exercised any date until expiration) to European style (can only be exercised at expiration), the expiration date (not within three days of normal expiration), as well as the strike price.

These options are exchange traded, so they are subject to competitive bid/offer markets from all crowd participants. The OCC prices options daily, letting managers obtain valuations for their risk management systems. FLEX options are backed by the options exchange and OCC, reducing the risk of counterparty failure.

FLEX options are exchange traded and backed by the OCC, so they may be used to offset margin requirements or other capital demands. OTC products are not quoted or backed by an independent third party, so they may not qualify for risk-offsetting valuations.

An institution holding OTC put options on the S&P 500 Index (SPX) in September 2008, for instance, was not able to use those contracts to offset a long position in index shares. The clearing firm failed to use those contracts as a bona fide hedge, because they lacked OCC backing and had no pricing. The fund had to put up additional capital for the margin transactions on the shares, as the options' value was quickly deteriorating. Funds can benefit by using FLEX contracts as an alternative that still fulfills the need for tailored derivatives products.

CHAPTER 13

The Changing Environment

THE WORLD IS ALWAYS CHANGING, and rules change with it. Companies that manage or handle investor capital have had to change their operating procedures and know more about their funds and their clients, in part because of credit review committees and regulations that combat money laundering.

The credit and liquidity crisis put credit lines under increasing scrutiny. Capital requirements and risk profiles have changed. Many managers deleveraged positions between 2007 and 2009, making it increasingly difficult for managers to achieve higher relative returns and compete with other funds. Added risk controls and monitoring have increased costs and have managers closing positions earlier than before.

These changes have actually helped the options market a bit. New rules have made some positions extremely risky, and these have been reduced or eliminated. The original methods of providing risk control and increasing manageability for standardized option contracts are in vogue again. Some managers have returned to hedging individual positions or portfolios, or are substituting options for stocks.

Managers are using long call options instead of long stock positions, which gives them more leverage. Borrowing is more expensive, and options are a cheaper alternative. This is especially true for higher-priced stocks, where option contracts provide more leverage and require relatively less capital.

Purchasing put contracts is becoming an alternative to selling shares short. Pending regulatory changes will probably include a reinstatement of some version of the uptick rule, which requires that every short sale be entered at a price that is higher than the price of the previous trade. That rule prevents short sellers from adding to the downward momentum, especially when a stock's price is in sharp decline and helps make the case for using puts instead of short stock positions. Once again, managers get more leverage from using long puts, and short call margin rules require less capital than do stock positions. Options can be less risky, too. Losses are limited to the put's cost, no matter how high the stock moves.

More and more managers are using technical analysis to determine risk levels and find potential changes in business and/or economic conditions that might affect their portfolios—before the companies themselves feel any impact. Technical strategists may also advise managers on changes in options activity, implied volatility, and insider transactions: all possible ways to work with changes.

Controlling Risk, Fixing Problems

There is no way to completely protect against failure. However, there are ways to mitigate problems and control risk. Repair strategies can help provide some disaster management without risking additional capital.

Managers may not be able to close positions, even if those holdings have losses with further deterioration. In fact, fund mandates may require that managers take additional positions, averaging down the cost of ownership and breaking even at a lower level. This may take a long time or may not happen at all.

It took IBM almost 10 years to return to pre-crash levels after the 1987 crash. The stock traded at nearly $44 (adjusted basis) in July 1987 and dropped to a low of $25.50 in October of that year. The stock moved relatively sideways for several years before declining to a low of $10.16 in August 1993, then turning higher. This stock was a widely held benchmark leader. Buying additional shares would have tied up capital for years and meant high portfolio interest costs.

IBM is an extreme case. (See Figure 13.1.) Most stocks, especially market leaders, do not sink for so long, particularly when other benchmarks are recovering. This extreme situation, however, shows that constant price averaging can take a long time to pay off. The capital

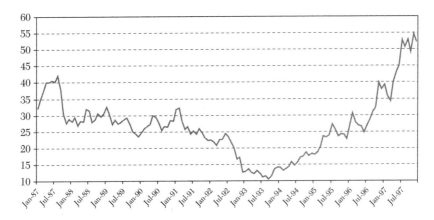

Figure 13.1 Monthly chart on International Business Machines (IBM) from 1987 to 1997. Note how long it took for the stock to return to the levels it held before the 1987 crash.

managers used to expand this position was expensive—and might have purchased other, profitable positions.

Flexibility is one of options' advantages. By combining a losing stock position with some strategic creations, we can often create repair strategies that change the break-even point without putting additional capital at risk.

Take First Solar Inc. (FSLR), an alternative energy company, as an example. The stock tends to rally when new developments, such as sharp energy price increases or tax incentive legislation, attract speculators and would-be investors. The shares set a double top (marginally lower high) in May and turned lower, dropping nearly 44 percent in three months (Figure 13.2). A July rally created a negative reversal pattern, which ultimately failed.

Imagine that you purchased 50,000 shares near $148 during the July rally. Shares are now at $116 and you have an unrealized loss of $32 per share, or 21.6 percent. Your team expects another rally as winter approaches and oil prices rise; they want to buy another 50,000 shares, putting another $5.8 million at risk and averaging the cost down to $132 per share. Your team would then have $13.2 million at risk on one stock.

Most managers would not only try to break even, but also to limit capital risk. Most repair strategies involve purchasing a 1-by-2 bullish ratio spread with several months until expiration. Managers buy a call with

Figure 13.2 First Solar Inc. (FSLR) daily chart. Note the double-top formation that led to a correction, only to be followed by a rally that turned into a negative reversal pattern.

a low, usually at-the-money strike price and sell two contracts against it with the same expiration date and a higher, usually out-of-the-money strike price.

The relationship between the stock price and the strike price depends on the issue price and the cost basis. Run the numbers on several scenarios or consult your options strategist before choosing a transaction. Ideally, the sold options pay for the purchased options, eliminating or minimizing additional capital risk.

Let's look at an example for FSLR. December calls with an at-the-money strike price of $115 are trading at $15.10. Calls with a $130 strike price are trading at $9.20. We own 50,000 shares, so we must purchase 500 of the December $115 calls and sell 1,000 of the December 130 calls to yield a net credit of $3.30 per share ($9.20 × 2 – $15.10). Our account has a credit of $165,000, because the spread is done on a 500-by-1,000 basis. (Options and stock must be kept in a margin account.)

Once the strategy is initiated we have two ways to prevent exposure to short-call option risk: a covered call and a bull spread.

Covered Call	**Bull Spread**
+ 50,000 FSLR	+ 500 FSLR Dec 115 Calls
− 500 FSLR Dec 130 Calls	− 500 FSLR Dec 130 Calls

Ideally, the stock rises to the upper strike price, maximizing the strategy. If FSLR rose back to $130:

Position	Gain/Loss (per share)	Total
Covered Write (stock cost at $148)	–$18	–$900,000
Bull Spread (theoretical max value)	$15	$750,000
Net Credit from Transaction	$ 3.30	$ 165,000
Anticipated Dividends	$ 0.00	$ 0
Net Gain/Loss	**$ 0.30**	**$ 15,000**

If the repair strategy works well, it generates a $15,000 profit, excluding transaction and interest charges, without putting any additional capital at risk. This strategy may be appropriate when market conditions abruptly change.

Table 13-1 shows a comparison of the three strategies based on five point intervals between $100 and $190.

Stock at Expiration	Per Share			Total Position		
	Repair Strategy	Average Down	No Action	Repair Strategy	Average Down	No Action
100	–44.7	–32	–48	–2,235,000	–3,200,000	–2,400,000
105	–39.7	–27	–43	–1,985,000	–2,700,000	–2,150,000
110	–34.7	–22	–38	–1,735,000	–2,200,000	–1,900,000
115	–29.7	–17	–33	–1,485,000	–1,700,000	–1,650,000
120	–19.7	–12	–28	–985,000	–1,200,000	–1,400,000
125	–9.7	–7	–23	–485,000	–700,000	–1,150,000
130	0.3	–2	–18	15,000	–200,000	–900,000
135	0.3	3	–13	15,000	300,000	–650,000
140	0.3	8	–8	15,000	800,000	–400,000
145	0.3	13	–3	15,000	1,300,000	–150,000
150	0.3	18	2	15,000	1,800,000	100,000
155	0.3	23	7	15,000	2,300,000	350,000

(continued)

Stock at Expiration	Per Share			Total Position		
	Repair Strategy	Average Down	No Action	Repair Strategy	Average Down	No Action
160	0.3	28	12	15,000	2,800,000	600,000
165	0.3	33	17	15,000	3,300,000	850,000
170	0.3	38	22	15,000	3,800,000	1,100,000
175	0.3	43	27	15,000	4,300,000	1,350,000
180	0.3	48	32	15,000	4,800,000	1,600,000
185	0.3	53	37	15,000	5,300,000	1,850,000
190	0.3	58	42	15,000	5,800,000	2,100,000

Using Global Markets

As the world has become increasingly interconnected, events that affect one part of the globe also reverberate in other places. Fund managers commonly own positions in foreign companies and markets, increasing their global exposure and risk. Managers can also use global markets to preserve or rescue positions when market conditions change.

U.S. markets are typically the most liquid, efficient, and transparent. They also have the greatest number of exchange-traded products. Using the U.S. markets to hedge global positions may be a practical choice, especially during periods of abnormal market activity.

Exchange-traded funds, American depository receipts, other share equivalents, and indices may help managers create offsetting positions or repair strategies in U.S. markets when other markets are closed or when executing in foreign markets is difficult. U.S. markets can also be good places to run strategies during high-volume periods, because U.S. markets typically clear transactions more efficiently.

Other benefits may include lower currency risk, a chance to avoid closed markets on foreign holidays, and opportunities to exploit time differences. For example, Israeli market trading occurs from Sunday to Thursday. Managers may benefit from trading in the United States when market changes happen on Thursday night, Friday, or Saturday. Managers with Japanese holdings could trade on U.S. exchanges when the Japanese markets close to observe various multiday holidays.

Commodity-related positions can also benefit from U.S. markets' electronic exchanges. News might push energy or hard metal prices upward, for instance, when physical markets are not in session. Electronic trades can help managers hedge or speculate against commodity-related companies.

Managers can use U.S. markets to reduce currency risk. Options and futures contracts are available on several exchanges, providing opportunities to hedge risk when managers are investing in different nations. Only major economic countries' currencies are typically available, which may affect the decision to invest in one nation over another. Some markets operate on an electronic basis—a plus for U.S. investors—and offer a wider range of hours than others.

Foreign currency options trade on two options exchanges: the International Securities Exchange (ISE) and the Philadelphia Stock Exchange (PHLX). Traders use calls and puts to hedge exposure to the major currencies. These contracts are not standardized in the same manner as equity and index options. They use different multipliers, premium calculations, and expirations. Their use and strategy creation go beyond the scope of this book, but managers should recognize them as another portfolio management tool.

CHAPTER 14

Using Options to Protect Capital

PROTECTING CAPITAL IS ONE of a fund manager's most crucial functions. Hedging techniques that use options to protect positions can help managers increase profits and attract new capital while also minimizing risk.

What Doesn't Work

That's not to say that every options strategy is a good hedge. Exchange-traded funds (ETFs) can indeed be part of risk management solutions. Leveraged, inverse, and leveraged inverse ETFs, however, are typically not good risk management vehicles, in my opinion. Some of these products have properties that *ought* to produce higher gains in a bull market, or appreciate in value as corresponding portfolios decline. But many managers have encountered problems with these ETFs, because these ETFs are rebalanced each evening—making them poor longer-term hedges—or because the hedge can't keep up with market activity. This has prompted lawmakers and regulators to take deeper looks at these products; some firms have restricted access to them.

In addition, there may be some problems with these ETFs with respect to margin practices. Purchasing an inverse or leveraged inverse ETF registers as a virtually long position on account books, so an extra short position could look like a long position, deceiving some risk analysis systems. Ineffective risk analysis systems can create serious problems for funds and brokers.

Absolutely critical [handwritten marginal note]

Single Security Hedges

Understanding individual security hedges can help managers create pair strategies or hedge one stock against a group of equities.

Let's start with a single security. A single security hedge can be the most important hedge, depending on the portfolio, and can also be the most expensive. Individual stocks can break ranks with the market because of a single news or corporate event, which may quickly drive shares sharply higher or lower and sometimes also dramatically increase trading volume. It's relatively easy to hedge individual stocks with relatively low implied volatility and option premiums. If the share price fails to appreciate and the hedge must be reimplemented over and over, however, the cost of that protection may counter any potential gain. A volatility skew is a useful tool in this situation, as it indicates whether option premiums are relatively cheap or expensive over a given period of time.

Figure 14.1 shows a hypothetical stock's at-the-money implied volatility reading, with options expiring in 30 to 720 days. The current reading is very high, at 43.50 percent; the 90-day reading declines to 39.21 percent. Volatility levels decrease over time, approaching 35 percent over the next two years. Traders and investors believe risk levels are relatively high now, but they think time will smooth out some of the risk.

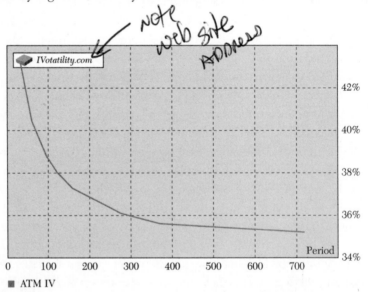

Figure 14.1 Courtesy of iVolatility.com. Note the sharp decline in implied volatility/ option premiums between the spot month and the two-year forecast.

(This stock has relatively high volatility to begin with, as it combines aspects of technology, retailing, and finance.)

Implied volatility is typically higher for spot-month contracts, because their values are more affected by short-term movements than are those of longer-term contracts. (We see a similar effect in moving averages, where shorter time periods show more reaction than their longer-term counterparts if the underlying share price moves sharply.)

Figure 14.2, which shows data from a technology/computer hardware company, is nearly the opposite of Figure 14.1. This stock is also generally more volatile than the broader equities market. The data, however, show that traders think the stock will be relatively calm over the next two or three months, with greater volatility risk later on. This may be due to seasonal factors or an anticipated event. The stock has traded in a narrow range for the past nearly four months (see Figure 14.3); traders likely believe that any movement, up or down, will be muted during the next few months.

As Figure 14.2 shows, implied volatility for options near expiration is 30.67 percent. At 180 days the reading is 33.25 percent: only a few points difference, but an 8.4 percent change. An 8.4 percent premium price increase can be substantial, especially on a higher price stock.

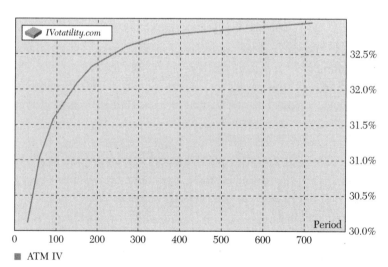

Figure 14.2 Courtesy of iVolatility.com. Note the sharp increase in implied volatility/ option premiums from the spot month forecasted out for two years.

Figure 14.3 Courtesy of Bloomberg LP. Note the relatively narrow trading range over the previous four months. This stock has a slightly positive trend but remains constrained by the top set the previous November.

Premium levels will affect the hedge type you choose. The easiest and quickest hedge is the purchase of an at-the-money or out-of-the-money put contract, but it involves a tradeoff between the price you can pay and the amount of downside risk you're willing to accept. The stock's sector or industry group, your earnings and news expectations, dividend payments, economic outlook, and market expectations may all influence your decision.

Purchasing an at-the-money put normally provides little downside risk, but the break-even point may be lower if premiums are high. Look at a range of puts and calculate the break-even points for purchasing contracts.

Run the numbers considering the impact of stock price changes at expiration. Doing so offers perspective on options only—potentially different from a view that includes stock, especially if the shares were purchased at a different price or over a series of prices.

In-the-money contracts provide higher delta values; the correlation between stock price moves and option price changes is higher. In-the-money contracts may be expensive because of their high intrinsic value, making it more difficult to profit from any upward movement. Deep in-the-money contracts further diminish leverage quality.

An at-the-money contract usually holds the largest time premium, in dollar terms, but that value is normally less than the intrinsic value of the in-the-money contract. At-the-money puts typically have delta readings between 40 percent and 55 percent, so the put's effectiveness over a 1-point stock price slide will give a potential recapture of between 40 percent and 55 percent. These contracts may not provide strong protection over the next point or two, but given the cost offset, they are probably the best hedge vehicles.

Out-of-the-money puts generally provide protection against a severe share price decline. Some people categorize this as "catastrophic protection," hedging against a significant decline in the share price. The cost of these options is relatively low, but they usually have a low delta, too. This means that they may offer little or no real protection during the first several points of a decline.

Procter & Gamble (PG)—Put Hedge Comparison

There are some interesting points in Table 14.1, which details various option contracts along with some of their valuations. Implied volatility ranges from a low of 18.01 percent to 22.79 percent, a range of 26.5 percent between the lowest and highest contracts. Deltas ranged between 0.22 and 0.76 in a single month, and the percentages that must be lost or gained to reach a break-even point ranged from a low of 1.6 percent to a high of 7.9 percent, also a large difference (and one that demonstrates the importance of analysis in choosing the right contracts).

Table 14.1 allows managers to evaluate choices and judge which contract would be best for them. This sample includes one in-the-money and one out-of-the-money contract in each month to simplify the choices. Your chart might also include theta measurements to illustrate the time decay over the next few days.

Most managers would avoid the 32-day contracts, since those contracts would be more expensive than the two-month contracts. Buying a short-term contract may also mean buying options frequently in order to maintain a hedge.

Conservative managers who want minimum losses at a manageable cost would likely purchase the three-month puts with the $55 strike, resulting in a break-even point that is 5.2 percent below the current stock price. This provides some downward risk, compensated by the increased time of 28 days.

Slightly more aggressive managers might purchase the two-month puts with a $55 strike, resulting in a break-even point of 4.3 percent below the current value. These managers might anticipate a rise in share prices over the next month or two, but still want a hedge against a potential market decline. Managers who want to protect against a sharp decline would purchase the three-month puts with a $52.50 strike.

Protective puts work well, especially when premiums are relatively low. They can offer reasonable potential premium losses, effective protection, and continued upside opportunities. But premiums are not always so accommodating. A collar strategy, which limits both downside risk and upside potential, is the next hedge strategy to consider.

Collar Hedges for Long Stock Positions

A collar, also referred to as a "hedge wrapper," lets a manager purchase a protective put with high implied volatility levels by also writing an out-of-the-money call; the call helps compensate for the hedge's cost. Managers who use this technique must believe that the share price will remain between the put's strike price and the call's strike price. They want to protect against a breakdown—so much that they are willing to sacrifice the upward potential for the stock should it rise above the call strike price.

Some managers use this strategy when they're not expecting market-moving news, but want to protect their holdings while they travel. Some managers use this strategy seasonally; others use it as protection against an upcoming earnings report or other, potentially negative news. In each case, the manager is willing to sell the position within a range on either side of the current market price during the remaining lifespan of those contracts.

Consider JC Penney (JCP), which was trading at $29.62 on a late-July afternoon in 2009. Retail stocks had enjoyed impressive appreciation, rallying to a high of $32.80 on May 5 after a March 6 low of $13.71. After the May high, the stock had gone into a consolidation period, with concerns about upcoming back-to-school sales and the holiday shopping period getting media attention.

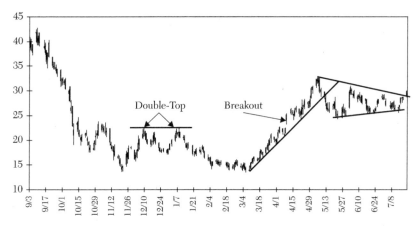

Figure 14.4 An 11-month daily Japanese candlestick chart on JC Penney (JCP).

A customer purchased shares following a break in the December–January double top (see Figure 14.4) and was concerned about the potential for a decline. Implied volatility levels had declined to near their 52-week lows for the 30-day to 60-day period, but were higher for the more distant future. The manager wanted to protect against a significant holiday downturn, but put premiums exceeded 10 percent of the stock price. This significantly reduces the effectiveness of the protected put strategy hedge. He was willing to sell his shares slightly above recent highs near $30, which would have resulted in a return of nearly 30 percent from his purchase price of $26.92.

Of these options, the best is likely purchasing the $27 January puts at $2.95 while selling the 32-1/2 January calls at $2.60 for a $0.35 net debit. The strategy means a small loss on the downside, but the upside potential would meet the manager's parameters. Table 14.2 illustrates the strategy, broken into its parts; Figure 14.5 graphically interprets the strategy.

JCP Collar Hedge Strategy—Value and P&L Analysis

Collar strategies are often popular with traders who like to sell volatility and find a barrier when attempting to buy a hedge in the face of higher option premiums. Although the collar keeps expectations range bound, it helps to minimize downside risk. The goal is to protect

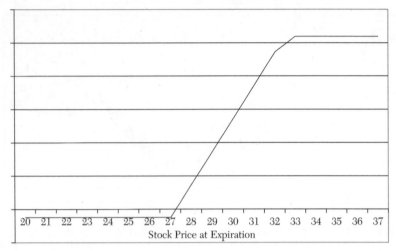

Stock Price at Expiration

Figure 14.5 Profit/loss illustration of the JCP collar strategy detailed in Table 14.2.

the asset against a quick, sharp decline. The holder must be willing to give up some upside potential in order to put protection in place. As with any investment decision, the balance of risk and reward will dominate the strategy's potential success.

Other Hedges for Offsetting High Volatility Levels

There are other strategies, too, that traders can use to offset higher implied volatility levels.

Traders who want to purchase a hedge should consider a bear spread that uses puts to help offset the cost of an at-the-money put contract. By using this strategy, managers can purchase protection without capping the stock's upside potential—a significant advantage. But this strategy also involves a limited downside hedge, which gives only partial protection if the stock drops sharply below the put's strike value. Some traders use this strategy only on stocks with low historic volatility; others say that its use depends on the price of the underlying shares.

By purchasing an at-the-money put, then selling an out-of-the-money put, managers hedge against a potential loss. The hedge's value is limited to the difference between the two strike prices. Once the lower strike price is penetrated, losses begin to mount again, unless the investor closes the position. The manager applies the sold put's premium against the purchased put's premium. Selling the out-of-the-money contract allows the manager to apply the premium against the cost of the purchased option, which reduces some of the inflated implied volatility found at the at-the-money strike price.

As an example, look at XYZ, a hypothetical transportation stock trading at $76.16. We want to hedge the long position that we purchased four months ago at $65.25. The company will report earnings in two days, and we suspect that results will disappoint the market, though we think that the stock will fall no lower than $70 if it does drop. Implied volatility for the current month is 36.49 percent.

To hedge this position, buy the one-month put with a $75 strike for $3.20 and sell the one-month put with the $70 strike for $2.05, creating a bear spread with a $1.15 net debit. If the stock drops below the $75 strike, the put's value will likely rise, helping to offset the share value loss. If the shares drop below the $70 strike, however, the strategy's effectiveness may be limited. The spread offers a benefit, but it is limited by the sold contract's strike price. If the stock's value rises, the hedge cost will likely offset any immediate gain.

Many strategies suggest new ideas, and this one is no exception. To hedge a position but reduce the hedge's cost, consider a ratio spread that involves purchasing one put contract for each 100 shares of the underlying stock that the position is long, then selling two contracts against each 100 shares.

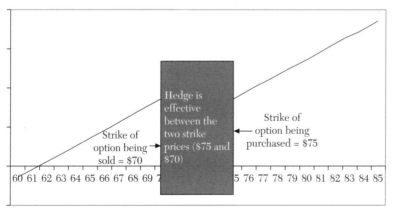

Figure 14.6 Analysis and profit/loss expected ability table for the bear spread using puts hedge.

This strategy includes a naked option—the extra sold put—which may be an advantage for a manager who wants to build a position on a price decline. In this sense, the strategy is similar to a low-limit buy order. The extra sold put contract, if assigned, will mean buying additional shares, adding to the position at a price that's lower than it was when the strategy was implemented.

But the strategy involves risk, too. Use the ratio spread, and you open yourself to the risk that the stock will drop below the sold put's strike price. The naked option (the extra sold put) will continue to appreciate as the shares decline, thus becoming a liability. The naked option is also subject to a margin requirement, and a fund must be approved for this strategy type, in addition to being approved to use spreads.

Using our previous example, let's analyze the ratio spread. Purchase one at-the-money contract with a $75 strike and sell two out-of-the-money contracts, each with a $70 strike, for a $0.90 net credit. The stock's upside potential remains unlimited, and the credit offsets the hedge cost. (This may not always be the case. Sometimes this strategy yields a small debit instead of a credit.)

This strategy's most effective point is at the lower strike price, where the options were sold. If the stock holds that price—$70 in this case—the sold puts expire worthless and the purchased put reaches its maximum value without an offset from the sold options.

If the shares continue to decline, however, the trade's profit/loss drops by two points—one for the stock and one for the naked put contract—for each point that the stock drops below the lower strike price. This risk has no downside cap.

Smart managers often use ratio spreads only within a month or two before option expiration. This helps limit downside liability and allows the fund to benefit from the options' time decay curve.

A put spread can also help managers create helpful strategies in high-volatility situations. Consider a $5 million portfolio that's strongly correlated to the NASDAQ 100 Index (NDX). The portfolio began with a value around $3.5 million and has grown nearly 43 percent over the past two years. The manager is concerned that a correction could erase some of those gains and hopes to use the PowerShares NASDAQ 100 Trust (QQQQ) to protect fund holdings against a potentially significant decline.

QQQQ is at $39.19 and the implied volatility for the end-of-quarter options, which have two months to expiration, is nearly 27 percent. Using

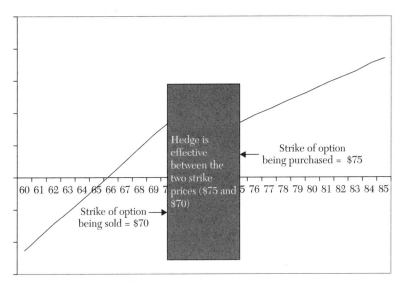

Hedge is effective between the two strike prices ($75 and $70)

Strike of option being purchased = $75

60 61 62 63 64 65 66 67 68 69 7 5 76 77 78 79 80 81 82 83 84 85

Strike of option being sold = $70

Figure 14.7 Profit/loss analysis on the stock when a put ratio spread hedges the downside.

a 95 percent correlation and the hedge calculation we outlined earlier, the manager should purchase 1,212 contracts.

The manager considers buying the $39 strike at $1.65 and selling the $33 strike against it for $0.45, for a net debit of $1.20 per share and a downside break-even point of $37.80. The portfolio must lose 3.5 percent before this strategy begins to work.

As an alternative, the manager considers buying 1,212 contracts and selling 2,424 contracts on a 1-by-2 ratio spread basis. Now the net debit drops to $0.75 per share and the break-even point becomes $38.25, or 2.4 percent below the current ETF price.

The ratio spread has two major disadvantages. First, it limits the downside to the sold put's lower striking price. Second, the strategy only begins to work, on a point-for-point basis, after breaking that lower strike price. In this example, the strategy's maximum effectiveness occurs at the $33 strike price, which is 15.8 percent below QQQQ's current price. At that point the portfolio would have lost approximately $750,000, with a spread worth six points, or $727,000 for the position. The gain would be $636,100 for a recapture rate of 84.8 percent.

Now comes the tricky part. For each point that QQQQ moves below the $33 strike price, the strategy gives back $121,200. Therefore, the second, downside break-even point is QQQQ at $27.76, down 29.2

percent from current levels. The fund loses $121,200 for each point QQQQ moves below that second break-even point.

This strategy can be very appealing, especially when option premiums and implied volatility levels are elevated. Remember, though, that high implied volatility levels are elevated for a reason, with real money behind the increase. The risk of the strategy may outweigh the benefits if the market drops 30 percent or more. Actively manage the position. If the market does not decline as time progresses, consider covering at least the naked portion of the ratio spread. This will also help free margin from the initial requirement.

Stock Replacement Therapy

The strategies we've discussed are all helpful in hedging single-stock positions. Stock replacement therapy, on the other hand, can work individually or in conjunction with an entire portfolio.

To use stock replacement therapy, find a purchase that your fund made during the past six months that has appreciated significantly: between 10 and 50 percent or more, depending on market conditions. The stock has had a good run, but it may be ending its seasonally strong period—or perhaps its appreciation rate is slowing. You wonder about more favorable opportunities, but you still want to maintain a position in this stock, in case the positive trend continues.

By selling the shares and replacing the stock with an in-the-money or at-the-money call contract, you remove the original capital commitment, plus the majority of the unrealized profits. But you still hold a position that will allow you to continue participating in any upside movement, and you limit your downside risk to the call premium paid.

Consider an example. Figure 14.8 shows weekly data on International Business Machines (IBM). The stock has been outperforming the market, rising from a low in November while the broad market continued to decline. Following a short correction in late June to early July, the stock broke out on volume following a positive earnings report, reaching a nine-month high that had it up 68.3 percent from its lows and up 40.9 percent from a March double-bottom.

For this example, assume that you purchased the stock at $90.54 and the shares are now at $117.02. Your fund has an unrealized gain of $26.48 per share, or 29.2 percent. You think the trend may end or a severe correction may be in the future.

You should consider selling the stock and buying a two-month call with a $115 strike for $5.30. The delta on this option is 61 percent, so at the next 1-point increase, the call's price will appreciate 61 cents. If the stock rises another 20 percent (to approximately $140) between now and expiration, the option's value will be $25 per share, or $2,500 for the contract. If the stock only rises 10 percent (to approximately $129), the option will be worth $14 per share, or $1,400 per contract. The gains would be $23 and $12, respectively, for a stock position. If the stock declines below the $155 strike price, the total exposure will be $5.30 for the contract.The following six tables can be used to evaluate different strategies for hedging positions.

At-the-Money Implied Volatility Skew #1

Table 14.1 Courtesy of iVolatility.com. Note the Sharp Decline in Implied Volatility/ Option Premiums between the Spot Month and the Three Month Contracts Forecast

Days to Expire	Strike	Bid	Offer	IV	Delta	BE Pt.	% to BE	Description
32	57.5	2.75	2.80	18.02	−0.76	54.70	1.55	One month in-the-money.
32	55.0	1.20	1.30	19.27	−0.47	53.70	3.35	One month at-the-money.
32	52.5	0.45	0.50	21.47	−0.22	52.00	6.41	One month out-of-the-money.
60	57.5	3.10	3.30	18.01	−0.68	54.20	2.45	Two month in-the-money.
60	55.0	1.75	1.85	20.40	−0.47	53.15	4.34	Two month at-the-money
60	52.5	0.90	1.00	22.14	−0.29	51.50	7.31	Two month out-of-the-money.
88	57.5	3.60	3.70	20.28	−0.64	53.80	3.17	Three month in-the-money.
88	55.0	2.20	2.30	21.10	−0.47	52.70	5.15	Three month at-the-money.
88	52.5	1.30	1.35	22.79	−0.31	51.15	7.94	Three month out-of-the-money.

At-the-Money Implied Volatility Skew #2

Table 14.2 Courtesy of iVolatility.com. Note the Sharp Increase in Implied Volatility/ Option Premiums from the Spot Month Forecasted Out for Two Years

Stock Price At Expiration	Stock P/L	Call Value	Call P/L	Put Value	Put P/L	Net Value	Net P/L
20	−6.92	0	2.6	7	4.05	27	−0.27
21	−5.92	0	2.6	6	3.05	27	−0.27
22	−4.92	0	2.6	5	2.05	27	−0.27
23	−3.92	0	2.6	4	1.05	27	−0.27
24	−2.92	0	2.6	3	0.05	27	−0.27
25	−1.92	0	2.6	2	−0.95	27	−0.27
26	−0.92	0	2.6	1	−1.95	27	−0.27
27	0.08	0	2.6	0	−2.95	27	−0.27
28	1.08	0	2.6	0	−2.95	28	0.73
29	2.08	0	2.6	0	−2.95	29	1.73
30	3.08	0	2.6	0	−2.95	30	2.73
31	4.08	0	2.6	0	−2.95	31	3.73
32	5.08	0	2.6	0	−2.95	32	4.73
33	6.08	0.5	2.1	0	−2.95	33.5	5.23
34	7.08	1.5	1.1	0	−2.95	35.5	5.23
35	8.08	2.5	0.1	0	−2.95	37.5	5.23
36	9.08	3.5	−0.9	0	−2.95	39.5	5.23
37	10.08	4.5	−1.9	0	−2.95	41.5	5.23

Table 14.3 Courtesy of Bloomberg LP. Note the relatively narrow trading range over the previous four months. This stock has a slightly positive trend but remains constrained by the top set on January 6

Days to Expire	Strike	Bid	Offer	IV	Delta	BE Pt.	% to BE	Description
32	57.5	2.75	2.80	18.02	−0.76	54.70	1.55	One month in-the-money.
32	55.0	1.20	1.30	19.27	−0.47	53.70	3.35	One month at-the-money.
32	52.5	0.45	0.50	21.47	−0.22	52.00	6.41	One month out-of-the-money.

60	57.5	3.10	3.30	18.01	−0.68	54.20	2.45	Two month in-the-money.
60	55.0	1.75	1.85	20.40	−0.47	53.15	4.34	Two month at-the-money
60	52.5	0.90	1.00	22.14	−0.29	51.50	7.31	Two month out-of-the-money.
88	57.5	3.60	3.70	20.28	−0.64	53.80	3.17	Three month in-the-money.
88	55.0	2.20	2.30	21.10	−0.47	52.70	5.15	Three month at-the-money.
88	52.5	1.30	1.35	22.79	−0.31	51.15	7.94	Three month out-of-the-money.

Table 14.4 Put hedge comparison table shows an in-the-money, at-the-money, and out-of-the-money put contract for each of the next three expiration periods

Stock Price At Expiration	Stock P/L	Call Value	Call P/L	Put Value	Put P/L	Net Value	Net P/L
20	−6.92	0	2.6	7	4.05	27	−0.27
21	−5.92	0	2.6	6	3.05	27	−0.27
22	−4.92	0	2.6	5	2.05	27	−0.27
23	−3.92	0	2.6	4	1.05	27	−0.27
24	−2.92	0	2.6	3	0.05	27	−0.27
25	−1.92	0	2.6	2	−0.95	27	−0.27
26	−0.92	0	2.6	1	−1.95	27	−0.27
27	0.08	0	2.6	0	−2.95	27	−0.27
28	1.08	0	2.6	0	−2.95	28	0.73
29	2.08	0	2.6	0	−2.95	29	1.73
30	3.08	0	2.6	0	−2.95	30	2.73
31	4.08	0	2.6	0	−2.95	31	3.73
32	5.08	0	2.6	0	−2.95	32	4.73
33	6.08	0.5	2.1	0	−2.95	33.5	5.23
34	7.08	1.5	1.1	0	−2.95	35.5	5.23
35	8.08	2.5	0.1	0	−2.95	37.5	5.23
36	9.08	3.5	−0.9	0	−2.95	39.5	5.23
37	10.08	4.5	−1.9	0	−2.95	41.5	5.23

Table 14.5 Strategy analysis for 1-by-2 ratio bear spread; Figure 14.6 illustrates the profit and loss analysis at expiration over a range of stock prices

Stock Price	Stock Profit/ Loss	At-the-Money Put Value	At-the-Money Profit/ Loss	Out-of-the-Money Put Value	Out-of-the-Money Profit/ Loss	Net Value	Net Profit/ Loss
60	−5.25	15.00	11.80	−10.00	−7.95	65.00	−1.40
61	−4.25	14.00	10.80	−9.00	−6.95	66.00	−0.40
62	−3.25	13.00	9.80	−8.00	−5.95	67.00	0.60
63	−2.25	12.00	8.80	−7.00	−4.95	68.00	1.60
64	−1.25	11.00	7.80	−6.00	−3.95	69.00	2.60
65	−0.25	10.00	6.80	−5.00	−2.95	70.00	3.60
66	0.75	9.00	5.80	−4.00	−1.95	71.00	4.60
67	1.75	8.00	4.80	−3.00	−0.95	72.00	5.60
68	2.75	7.00	3.80	−2.00	0.05	73.00	6.60
69	3.75	6.00	2.80	−1.00	1.05	74.00	7.60
70	4.75	5.00	1.80	0.00	2.05	75.00	8.60
71	5.75	4.00	0.80	0.00	2.05	75.00	8.60
72	6.75	3.00	−0.20	0.00	2.05	75.00	8.60
73	7.75	2.00	−1.20	0.00	2.05	75.00	8.60
74	8.75	1.00	−2.20	0.00	2.05	75.00	8.60
75	9.75	0.00	−3.20	0.00	2.05	75.00	8.60
76	10.75	0.00	−3.20	0.00	2.05	76.00	9.60
77	11.75	0.00	−3.20	0.00	2.05	77.00	10.60
78	12.75	0.00	−3.20	0.00	2.05	78.00	11.60
79	13.75	0.00	−3.20	0.00	2.05	79.00	12.60
80	14.75	0.00	−3.20	0.00	2.05	80.00	13.60
81	15.75	0.00	−3.20	0.00	2.05	81.00	14.60
82	16.75	0.00	−3.20	0.00	2.05	82.00	15.60
83	17.75	0.00	−3.20	0.00	2.05	83.00	16.60
84	18.75	0.00	−3.20	0.00	2.05	84.00	17.60
85	19.75	0.00	−3.20	0.00	2.05	85.00	18.60

Table 14.6 Profit/loss analysis on the stock when the put spread using puts strategy is used to hedge the downside

Stock Price	Stock Profit/ Loss	At-the-Money Put Value	At-the-Money Profit/ Loss	Out-of-the-Money Put Value	Out-of-the-Money Profit/ Loss	Net Value	Net Profit/ Loss
60	−5.25	15.00	11.80	−10.00	−7.95	65.00	−1.40
61	−4.25	14.00	10.80	−9.00	−6.95	66.00	−0.40
62	−3.25	13.00	9.80	−8.00	−5.95	67.00	0.60
63	−2.25	12.00	8.80	−7.00	−4.95	68.00	1.60
64	−1.25	11.00	7.80	−6.00	−3.95	69.00	2.60
65	−0.25	10.00	6.80	−5.00	−2.95	70.00	3.60
66	0.75	9.00	5.80	−4.00	−1.95	71.00	4.60
67	1.75	8.00	4.80	−3.00	−0.95	72.00	5.60
68	2.75	7.00	3.80	−2.00	0.05	73.00	6.60
69	3.75	6.00	2.80	−1.00	1.05	74.00	7.60
70	4.75	5.00	1.80	0.00	2.05	75.00	8.60
71	5.75	4.00	0.80	0.00	2.05	75.00	8.60
72	6.75	3.00	−0.20	0.00	2.05	75.00	8.60
73	7.75	2.00	−1.20	0.00	2.05	75.00	8.60
74	8.75	1.00	−2.20	0.00	2.05	75.00	8.60
75	9.75	0.00	−3.20	0.00	2.05	75.00	8.60
76	10.75	0.00	−3.20	0.00	2.05	76.00	9.60
77	11.75	0.00	−3.20	0.00	2.05	77.00	10.60
78	12.75	0.00	−3.20	0.00	2.05	78.00	11.60
79	13.75	0.00	−3.20	0.00	2.05	79.00	12.60
80	14.75	0.00	−3.20	0.00	2.05	80.00	13.60
81	15.75	0.00	−3.20	0.00	2.05	81.00	14.60
82	16.75	0.00	−3.20	0.00	2.05	82.00	15.60
83	17.75	0.00	−3.20	0.00	2.05	83.00	16.60
84	18.75	0.00	−3.20	0.00	2.05	84.00	17.60
85	19.75	0.00	−3.20	0.00	2.05	85.00	18.60

Table 14.7 The values and profit/loss analysis for this strategy.; Figure 14.7 offers a graphic depiction. There is little difference between this chart and Figure 14.6, except that the scale has changed to reflect the additional loss potential and the decline of the slope is steeper

Stock Price	Stock Profit/ Loss	At-the-Money Put Value	Profit/ Loss	Out-of-the-Money Put Value	Profit/ Loss	Net Value	Net Profit/ Loss
60	−5.25	15.00	11.80	−20.00	−17.95	55.00	−11.40
61	−4.25	14.00	10.80	−18.00	−15.95	57.00	−9.40
62	−3.25	13.00	9.80	−16.00	−13.95	59.00	−7.40
63	−2.25	12.00	8.80	−14.00	−11.95	61.00	−5.40
64	−1.25	11.00	7.80	−12.00	−9.95	63.00	−3.40
65	−0.25	10.00	6.80	−10.00	−7.95	65.00	−1.40
66	0.75	9.00	5.80	−8.00	−5.95	67.00	0.60
67	1.75	8.00	4.80	−6.00	−3.95	69.00	2.60
68	2.75	7.00	3.80	−4.00	−1.95	71.00	4.60
69	3.75	6.00	2.80	−2.00	0.05	73.00	6.60
70	4.75	5.00	1.80	0.00	2.05	75.00	8.60
71	5.75	4.00	0.80	0.00	2.05	75.00	8.60
72	6.75	3.00	−0.20	0.00	2.05	75.00	8.60
73	7.75	2.00	−1.20	0.00	2.05	75.00	8.60
74	8.75	1.00	−2.20	0.00	2.05	75.00	8.60
75	9.75	0.00	−3.20	0.00	2.05	75.00	8.60
76	10.75	0.00	−3.20	0.00	2.05	76.00	9.60
77	11.75	0.00	−3.20	0.00	2.05	77.00	10.60
78	12.75	0.00	−3.20	0.00	2.05	78.00	11.60
79	13.75	0.00	−3.20	0.00	2.05	79.00	12.60
80	14.75	0.00	−3.20	0.00	2.05	80.00	13.60
81	15.75	0.00	−3.20	0.00	2.05	81.00	14.60
82	16.75	0.00	−3.20	0.00	2.05	82.00	15.60
83	17.75	0.00	−3.20	0.00	2.05	83.00	16.60
84	18.75	0.00	−3.20	0.00	2.05	84.00	17.60
85	19.75	0.00	−3.20	0.00	2.05	85.00	18.60

Figure 14.8 International Business Machines (IBM) weekly chart with relative performance vs. the S&P 500 Index (dotted line). Notice how the stock is outperforming the broader large-cap market. Can it keep rising to the highs near $130? That would be another 11.1 percent appreciation.

Capital preservation is one of the most important tenets with respect to increasing alpha. Managers who consistently allow their portfolios to be at risk can be jeopardizing their futures, the future of the fund they are managing, and the welfare of their investors/clients. Taking proactive measures, such as the strategies we have reviewed in this Chapter, can make the world of difference in overall performance. Additionally, by showing investors the work that went into management of their portfolio/fund, clients can increase capital investment as they tell friends and family how their manager worked for them.

CHAPTER 15

Hedging the Broad Portfolio

UNDERSTANDING THE STRATEGIES to this point could help a manager in paired trades—also called uncorrelated trades--between a group or portfolio and a single stock. Figure 15.1 shows the relationship between risk/reward and volatility in hedging long stock positions.

Many managers, of course, also need to hedge entire portfolios.

Portfolio hedging falls into one of two categories, with different hedge types effective in each. The first category is broad, focusing on a base that crosses two or more sectors. It is not sector specific and has a high correlation with broad market movements. The second category,

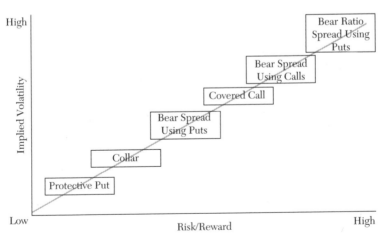

Figure 15.1 Long stock hedging strategies that are based on implied volatility/option premium levels.

discussed in the next section, concentrates on portfolios that highly correlate to a sector or industry group.

Before exchange-traded funds gained popularity, strategists often used index options to hedge large portfolios. Commonly employed instruments included the S&P 500 Index (SPX), Russell 2000 Index (RUT), and S&P 400 Mid-Cap Index (MID). These indices can still be used today, but the ETF market's widespread acceptance has made products such as the S&P Depository Trust (SPY) and iSHARES Russell 2000 Index Fund (IWM) generally better choices for fund managers.

During the past several years the demand for ETFs has grown, in part because they are a fraction of their corresponding indices and therefore typically less expensive. ETFs contracts generally enjoy competitive pricing, as most are traded on multiple exchanges. Indices, by contrast, normally trade on just one exchange. Even following large market moves, a deep-in-the-money ETF usually costs less than a deep-in-the-money index. Traders also find it easier—and more liquid—to trade underlying ETF shares, compared to trading an entire index basket or futures.

Used as hedges, ETFs have several more advantages over indices. They allow a manager to tailor a hedge closer to the portfolio's value. And the holder can execute ETF options on any date before expiration, as these are American-style contracts. Most indices use European-style contracts, which limit exercise to the final trading day.

But ETF options aren't as good as index options if traders exercise a contract. Settle an ETF option contract, and you'll have to deliver the ETF shares. Note that this is not your portfolio but the shares of that corresponding ETF. Index options, by contrast, are settled in cash, which can be applied to or against portfolio value.

To create the general hedge, look for an index or ETF that has a high correlation with your portfolio. Choose the hedge period, but don't choose a contract that expires too quickly, as the time decay erodes the value. Next choose an at-the-money or slightly out-of-the-money strike price. Now comes the hard part: deciding how many put contracts to purchase. We use the formula:

$$\text{Number of Puts for Hedge} = \frac{(\text{portfolio value} \times \text{correlation})}{(\text{index or ETF value} \times 100)}$$

almost critical (handwritten margin note)

Consider illustrations using first an index, then an ETF hedge. A $10 million portfolio holds 70 securities that have a high correlation to SPX—in this example, a 90 percent correlation.

Using the formula, a current SPX reading of 957.16, and a SPY reading of 95.78, we find that we should purchase 94 SPX index puts or 940 SPY puts, respectively. The two-month, at-the-money puts have strike prices of 955 and 95, respectively. The SPX option premium is 35.70; the SPY contract costs 3.55. Therefore, the hedges cost $335,680.55 and $333,576.95, respectively. Excluding transaction charges, the difference between these two options is $2,103.60. For SPX, the hedge cost represents 3.4 percent of portfolio value. For SPY, the cost is 3.3 percent of the portfolio value.

Now consider the impact based on market movement with the final prices at expiration in two months (Table 15.1).

A look at Table 15.1 shows that, in this case, the SPX hedge is slightly more effective than the SPY hedge. Note that, if you attempted to sell the options contracts, the SPX contract would be worth $189 per share ($18,900 per contract) if the market were down 20 percent, compared to $18 per share ($1,800 per contract) for SPY. Considering market liquidity, it would probably be easier to sell SPY contracts. You could be forced to sell SPX contracts at a sharply discounted value or wait to exercise at expiration.

When I analyze hedges, I also look at the hedge's effectiveness based on the put contract's recapture rate compared to the portfolio loss. This tells me whether the hedge is worthwhile. As the market declines, a hedge's effectiveness should continue to rise above the portfolio loss. A 100 percent recapture rate is probably impossible, but recapture rates above 75 percent on a 20 percent portfolio decline are good.

Table 15.2 shows a portfolio evaluation that includes the gains or losses incurred by using SPX or SPY hedges. The first recapture rate, with the market down 5 percent, is fairly low, because the hedge cost is still being absorbed. That initial cost generally spreads out as the market declines, improving hedge viability. As the market declines and the put contracts are more in the money, the puts' delta will rise, making each 1-point drop more effective from a hedging standpoint. When the market is down 20 percent the SPX hedge has a recapture rate of 79.1 percent; SPY has a recapture rate of 77.4 percent.

Table 15.1 Comparison of hedging strategies using the SPX index and SPY ETF. The output has been truncated for editing purposes. The "Value" column is the approximate reading for the portfolio, SPX or SPY, where appropriate. Net values are the profit/loss of the hedge after the impact of the change in portfolio value. Computations are based on prices at expiration.

SPX Level	Portfolio			SPX				SPY		
	Value	Gain/Loss		Value	Gain/Loss	Net		Value	Gain/Loss	Net
1148.59+20%	11,800,000	1,800,000		1,149	−335,681	1,464,319		115	−333,577	1,466,423
1052.87+10%	10,900,000	900,000		1,053	−335,681	564,319		105	−333,577	566,423
1005.01+5%	10,450,000	450,000		1,005	−335,681	114,319		101	−333,577	116,423
957.16 Unch	10,000,000	0		957	−335,681	−335,681		96	−333,577	−333,577
909.30−5%	9,550,000	−450,000		909	73,881	−376,119		91	43,269	−406,731
861.44−10%	9,100,000	−900,000		861	523,746	−376,254		86	493,435	−406,565
765.72−20%	8,200,000	−1,800,000		766	1,423,476	−376,524		77	1,393,767	−406,233

Table 15.2 Comparison of projected recapture rates for hedges used in Table 15.1. Computations are based on prices at expiration

At Expiration	SPX Level	Portfolio Gain/Loss	SPX Hedge Gain/Loss	Recapture Rate	SPY Hedge Gain/Loss	Recapture Rate
SPX-5%	909.302	−450,000	73,881	16.4	43,269	9.6
SPX-10%	861.444	−900,000	523,746	58.2	493,435	54.8
SPX-20%	765.728	−1,800,000	1,423,476	79.1	1,393,767	77.4

Reducing Hedge Costs

The SPX generally has a higher recapture rate, but the cost of purchasing that hedge is nearly $2,100 more than the cost of SPY.

Higher implied volatility levels can sometimes make a portfolio hedging strategy more costly, diluting the value and potential recapture rate. This can happen at any time, but it is more common when the market has peaked or when some negative news or other event raises concerns. It is also more common near the end of summer when worries over a potential market correction increase. (September is historically the worst month of the year, with an average decline of 0.5 percent, though that decline doesn't happen every year. Furthermore, corrections can offer bulls opportunities.)

Increasing premiums can render a strategy pointless, because the hedge's cost may significantly affect recapture rates. Consider writing a call against the long put purchase with a strike that's above the current index level. This provides some additional upside potential without an immediate cap.

The seasonally weak period ending in October often ushers in a seasonal strong period in November. This is one reason that you may want to keep hedge length short: There's no sense in buying a hedge, only to see the market turn around and the strategy evaporate. Don't just protect capital—create opportunities, too.

If a market or stock drops significantly and you anticipate a recovery, begin selling part of the hedge position near your estimated low point. Keep working the hedge until you are convinced that a rebound is at hand, then close the remaining hedge position. This lets you record gains against your portfolio's unrealized losses, starting the next upward leg at a virtual level that's lower than the point at which the market began its decline. This will help improve performance and may provide additional capital for new positions.

The cost of a hedge can be self-defeating, especially when premiums are elevated. Higher implied volatility, especially when seasonal factors drive it, may produce hedges that are too expensive to be useful. A portfolio collar strategy may help reduce costs while still providing some upside potential. (The goal is to reduce the cost, but a very inexpensive or free solution may exist, depending on the relationship between the index/ETF and option strike prices.)

To see this strategy in action, consider an example: a hedge on a $2 million technology portfolio. The fund has been accumulating technology stocks for the past year and, given the appreciation, wants to hedge those shares against a market decline.

The Select Sector SPiDR—Technology ETF (XLK) is at $19.57. The portfolio has a 93 percent correlation with XLK, so an adequate hedge means buying 950 put contracts. Managers want a two-month hedge. The XLK September 19 puts cost $0.95, or 4.9 percent of the ETF's value. This may be too steep and thus ineffective, as a 10 percent drop would value XLK at $17.61.

In addition to purchasing puts, managers should consider selling the September 21 calls at $0.45 for a net strategy debit of $0.50. In essence, the move reduces the hedge cost by 47 percent while still giving the portfolio some upside potential to the $21 strike price, or the ability to appreciate another 7.3 percent before being capped. Table 15.3 shows the results from this trade; Figure 15.2 provides a graphic representation.

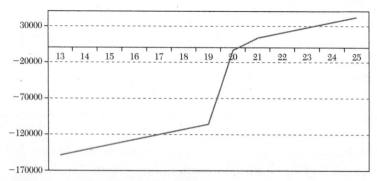

Figure 15.2 Illustration of XLK portfolio collar.

Table 15.3 XLK portfolio collar strategy evaluation—Note the accelerating recapture rate as the value of the portfolio declines. Results are priced at expiration

At Expiration	Portfolio Value	Change in Portfolio	Sep 19 Put Gain/Loss	Sep 21 Call Gain/Loss	Net Result	Recap Rate
25	2,554,931.02	554,931.02	-90,250.00	-422,750.00	41,931.02	
24	2,452,733.78	452,733.78	-90,250.00	-327,750.00	34,733.78	
23	2,350,536.54	350,536.54	-90,250.00	-232,750.00	27,536.54	
22	2,248,339.29	248,339.29	-90,250.00	-137,750.00	20,339.29	
21	2,146,142.05	146,142.05	-90,250.00	-42,750.00	13,142.05	
20	2,043,944.81	43,944.81	-90,250.00	42,750.00	-3,555.19	
19	1,941,747.57	-58,252.43	-90,250.00	42,750.00	-105,752.43	
18	1,839,550.33	-160,449.67	4,750.00	42,750.00	-112,949.67	29.6
17	1,737,353.09	-262,646.91	99,750.00	42,750.00	-120,146.91	54.3
16	1,635,155.85	-364,844.15	194,750.00	42,750.00	-127,344.15	65.1
15	1,532,958.61	-467,041.39	289,750.00	42,750.00	-134,541.39	71.2
14	1,430,761.37	-569,238.63	384,750.00	42,750.00	-141,738.63	75.1
13	1,328,564.13	-671,435.87	479,750.00	42,750.00	-148,935.87	77.8

Managers who are reluctant to write calls to offset put purchases could use a bear spread strategy instead. A ratio bear strategy may be a good choice for managers who think the market will decline only by a certain percentage. Regardless of your choice, writing an out-of-the-money put against a long put may reduce your cost.

Pairing Up

As we've discussed, selecting the right pair strategies while also looking for other opportunities, such as issues that rise in a falling market, can be a very lucrative strategy and often attracts managers from a variety of philosophical schools. Some fundamental analysts might believe that, despite a weak economy, a particular stock or sector will still continue to rise. Technical and quantitative analysts may also seek stocks that go against the grain, considering them defensive or relating their antici- pated performance to market or economic cycles. Hedges can augment good pair selections.

To see how, consider this scenario. Recent activity shows that prices are on the rise and certain commodities are scarce. The unemployment rate is near 5 1/2 percent and employers continue to compete for good hires, pushing wages upward. Following two years of accommodating monetary policy, the Federal Open Market Committee (FOMC) begins raising interest rates in response to increasing inflationary pressures. The FOMC announces that it will raise the federal discount rate and the federal funds target rate by 50 basis points each.

Anticipating this action, some portfolio managers have slowly begun using hedging strategies. They have also taken contrary positions in equities that correlate strongly with inflationary pressures, a group that includes commodity/metals and energy stocks. By overweighting or pur- chasing calls on these stocks, they may benefit from increasing demand for these companies or their products as the tightening cycle progresses.

When volatility levels are above average, writing out-of-the-money puts may result in minimal gains while also letting a fund benefit from the progression of time and option premium decay. Downside hedges help offset potential market contractions while long positions get a chance to increase in value, giving the fund manager market outperformance.

Other techniques may also prove useful. If interest rates are rising, a manager may purchase puts on companies related to construction or real estate in the belief that higher mortgage rates will disproportionately affect these companies. In addition to purchasing a portfolio hedge, a manager might also take a bearish position in the SPDR S&P Homebuilders ETF (XHB). Another manager may believe that higher interest rates are pinching consumers and so sell calls against the SPDR S&P Retail ETF (XRT).

These strategies can become multifaceted and confusing. Monitor the aggregate portfolio movement as well as the pieces. Look at relative performance and momentum as you draw trend lines. The options marketplace can provide intelligence on the pressure and activity behind implied volatility and premium levels.

Hedging Short Portfolios

Hedging long portfolios is important; hedging short positions is equally crucial. Many funds are both long and short, with paired-off long and short positions that managers hope will produce profits by moving in their desired respective directions. Other funds may also look for shorting opportunities and may need a hedge against a sudden upward movement.

The market tends to decline faster than it appreciates, but sometimes strong bull moves occur over a short period of time. Recent history provides a good example. In 2009 the S&P 500 Index (SPX) gained more than 50 percent, moving from its early-March lows of 666.70 to more than 1,000 in less than four months (Figure 15.3). This rise followed a slide from 1576.09, a loss of nearly 58 percent.

The advance on the right side of the chart took place without a meaningful correction. The largest decline occurred from mid-June to early July, which saw a 7.1 percent adjustment. Some strong periods, such as mid-May and mid-July, were partially due to traders covering shorts as bulls squeezed prices higher.

It is more difficult to hedge short positions than it is to hedge long positions, for two reasons. First, volatility generally rises as prices decline. As a result, managers may need to close profitable short positions prematurely when a hedge becomes too expensive. Second, short sellers can be bought in, which could significantly affect a short portfolio and invalidate the hedge.

More creative measures are in order. In most cases we would flip the hedges used for long portfolios, but high volatility could prevent

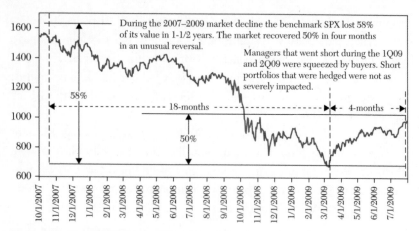

Figure 15.3 The S&P 500 Index (SPX) from October 2007 to July 2009. This daily chart shows the sharp decline and subsequent impressive recovery from the March lows.

us from purchasing a call option—at least initially. If the market has appreciated and implied volatility has dropped, buying a call might be a good hedging strategy. This strategy may also be a good alternative if the market has risen and you are moving out of one hedging strategy and into another.

For an example, imagine a short portfolio that's weighted to the Dow Jones Industrial Average (DJIA) and has a 92 percent negative correlation to that benchmark. Portfolio value is approximately $6 million. The Diamonds Trust (DIA), a reduced-value ETF of the DJIA, has a current value of $92.79. Our formula indicates that we need 595 contracts to hedge the position. Two-month calls with a $93 strike are trading at $2.50, so the hedge will cost $148,750 (excluding charges), or a reasonable 2.5 percent of portfolio value. The contract's implied volatility level is 21.42 percent. Table 15.4 illustrates the impact of a hedge on a short portfolio.

In this case, the recapture rate is nearly 72 percent with the market up 13 percent. This is similar to the simpler strategies that hedge long portfolios.

Now consider the situation a few months earlier, when the implied volatility was 43.54 percent and DIA was $66.50. The two-month call with a $67 strike cost $3.75. A lower market and higher volatility meant that an equivalent contract was nearly 2 percent more expensive. The

Table 15.4 Short portfolio hedge strategy—Evaluation of strategy over a range of values at options expiration

DIA = $92.79	Portfolio Value	Change in Portfolio	DIA 2-Month $93 Calls Gain/Loss	Net Result	Recapture Rate
85	6,503,718.07	503,718.07	−148,750.00	652,468.07	
86	6,439,055.93	439,055.93	−148,750.00	587,805.93	
87	6,374,393.79	374,393.79	−148,750.00	523,143.79	
88	6,309,731.65	309,731.65	−148,750.00	458,481.65	
89	6,245,069.51	245,069.51	−148,750.00	393,819.51	
90	6,180,407.37	180,407.37	−148,750.00	329,157.37	
91	6,115,745.23	115,745.23	−148,750.00	264,495.23	
92	6,051,083.09	51,083.09	−148,750.00	199,833.09	
93	5,986,420.95	−13,579.05	−148,750.00	135,170.95	
94	5,921,758.81	−78,241.19	−89,250.00	−167,491.19	
95	5,857,096.67	−142,903.33	−29,750.00	−172,653.33	
96	5,792,434.53	−207,565.47	29,750.00	−177,815.47	14.3
97	5,727,772.39	−272,227.61	89,250.00	−182,977.61	32.8
98	5,663,110.25	−336,889.75	148,750.00	−188,139.75	44.2
99	5,598,448.11	−401,551.89	208,250.00	−193,301.89	51.9
100	5,533,785.97	−466,214.03	267,750.00	−198,464.03	57.4
101	5,469,123.83	−530,876.17	327,250.00	−203,626.17	61.6
102	5,404,461.69	−595,538.31	386,750.00	−208,788.31	64.9
103	5,339,799.55	−660,200.45	446,250.00	−213,950.45	67.6
104	5,275,137.41	−724,862.59	505,750.00	−219,112.59	69.8
105	5,210,475.27	−789,524.73	565,250.00	−224,274.73	71.6

hedge would have been less effective and the short position would have suffered if the market had moved lower.

At this point, managers had several alternatives. A manager could implement an offsetting bull spread, selling an out-of-the-money call to offset the cost of the purchased call. Or a manager could sell an out-of-the-money put. Here, a two-month put with a $65 strike would have cost $3.52. Combine this strategy with the long call, using the short put to reduce the cost.

A manager could also close the short positions and swap them into long puts, short calls, or a combination. This would lessen the chances of being bought in and reduce any potential rebate for the short positions. The short-call premiums would also let a manager take advantage of the time premium deterioration. Consider implementing this strategy on a majority of the portfolio and using individual stock strategies for holdings with the greatest negative momentum and/or relative strength readings. Use trailing stops to limit reversal risk. Managers who combine these methods can expect to outperform the market, as the worst-declining outliers should fall faster than average.

Other Hedge Types

In addition to hedging against market movement, many managers hedge against moves caused by changes in other critical markets: commodities, energy, currencies, and interest rates.

It's hard to establish correlations between different markets, because the relationship between portfolios and ancillary markets often changes. (Sector-focused portfolios may be the exception; these may have consistently high correlations and can easily be hedged.)

In 2008, a severe real estate market downturn and an impending credit market crisis hurt financial firms. Crude oil prices were rising, climbing to an all-time high just below the $150 per barrel level, and many managers were concerned about the negative potential for the market or for their portfolios. They did not want to turn bearish, especially as energy holdings were benefiting from the increase, but they needed a hedge.

It's easy to hedge oil by using the US Oil Fund LP (USO), an ETF that has a very high correlation to light sweet crude oil futures. USO does not require a commodities/futures account and is an equity security traded on an equities exchange, with options available on several exchanges. These contracts help managers manage risk that's directly and indirectly related to crude oil price movements. Figure 15.4 shows the relationship between crude oil futures and USO.

Managers might also consider hedges that use the US Natural Gas Fund (UNG), another energy-related ETF. This fund is highly correlated to the

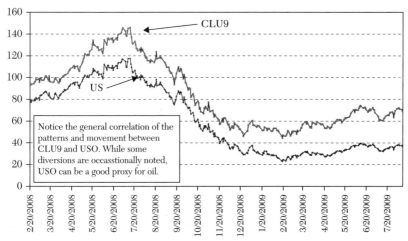

Figure 15.4 Crude Oil Futures vs. US Oil Fund LP (USO)—The patterns and movements between the two instruments are highly correlated, allowing managers to use USO as a proxy for oil when hedging positions.

price of natural gas and can move differently from its USO counterpart. Some managers create a pair trade, buying USO and selling UNG (or vice versa) when they anticipate divergence. Options contracts can help here as well, providing leverage and/or risk control.

Gold is another possible commodity hedge. Some managers consider it an inflationary indicator; others use it as a safe haven during periods of rising prices or political instability.

The SPDR Gold Trust (GLD) can help replicate gold price movement in an equity environment. The Market Vectors Gold Miners ETF (GDX) correlates with gold mining companies. Analysts might believe that gold miners will outperform the commodity, creating additional opportunities for both speculation and hedging.

Managers may also look to hedge against interest-rate changes, particularly for long portfolios when rates are expected to rise. Monetary policy changes can help or hurt stocks, but it's not always easy to predict the actual affect.

For an example, let's say that analysts think the Federal Reserve will increase the Fed funds rate by 25 basis points. The event is anticipated, so it may already be built into bond and stock prices. But committee comments may further affect the markets. Managers may want a hedge against further rate increases.

They might choose between several different instruments. Interest rate index options issued by the Chicago Board Options Exchange (CBOE) may provide a hedge. There are four related indices: the Short-term Interest Rate Index (IRX), the 5-Year Yield Index (FVX), the 10-Year Yield Index (TNX), and the 30-Year Yield Index (TYX). These indices are based on interest rates, not bond prices. Their pricing levels are 10 times the actual interest rate, which allows for trading options.

An ETF on the Barclays 20+ Year Treasury Bond Fund (TLT) is another popular instrument. This fund is based on price, not interest. Buy put options if you think interest rates are going higher, because the fund price typically moves lower when rates increase.

Monitor Your Holdings

As you create hedges, make sure that you include all your positions in your analysis. If you do not have a risk management system, create a rudimentary one. Develop a spreadsheet that shows current positions and values, as well as projected values based on market movements.

Figure net position values and consider charting the data to study the portfolio visually. Remember that not every position will move in step with the market, that projections are just for analytical purposes, and that option values will change with volatility and other variable factors. Use theoretical value calculations to increase projection accuracy, but remember that these assumptions may not be accurate.

CHAPTER 16

When to Invest,
When to Trade

WHAT'S THE DIFFERENCE BETWEEN investors and traders? Both buy and sell securities, looking to make the best possible profits. In some contexts, the terms investor and trader are used interchangeably. And *investors* and *traders* are well advised to understand and follow each other's strategies, as deep market knowledge helps every financial professional.

But there are some significant differences between these two professional descriptions, and markets that favor one or the other. Recognizing these differences can help managers avoid pitfalls and achieve alpha.

Investors and Investment Markets

Most investors try to purchase shares and hold them as long as possible, looking for the continued appreciation that will likely coincide with economic growth. In most instances, however, stocks lead the economy by three to six months or more, so many investors enter and exit their positions late.

The rising number of stocks trading above their 200-day moving averages confirmed rising major market benchmarks. This was a positive trend, one that investors could purchase and hold. Based on this indicator, I would have begun purchasing shares in May, following a break from the August highs, and taken a more aggressive position in June, after NYSEPAUS (Bloomberg symbol for NYSE shares above their 200-day moving averages) broke above the 50 percent level. Implied volatility levels were high at the time, so I suggested covered combinations and put writing as ways to help managers begin or enhance positions while reducing risk and taking advantage of high premiums.

When stocks are strong, the market often discounts bad news and rallies sharply on good news. In the end, however, what goes up must come down. Risk is still present, and no rally continues forever.

Trading an Investment Trend

Pay particular attention as the trend begins. This is generally the riskiest time to invest, though a new positive trend that follows a sharp negative trend or bear market may carry relatively low risk. If implied volatility levels are high, consider writing out-of-the-money put contracts instead of buying shares, to help balance risk and reward. The profit potential may be limited to the premium collected, with the risk that you may own the stock at a lower cost (put option strike price minus premium).

Managers could also buy a quarter position in the stock and sell an equivalent number of out-of-the-money calls and puts with between two and six months until expiration. For an example, XYZ is a stock trading at $39.17. It has an implied volatility around 150 percent. (The stock is attempting to break out from a base.) A manager might buy the stock, write/sell puts, or create a covered combination.

Buying the stock means putting the share cost at risk, but that strategy has the potential for unlimited gain. By selling puts we earn a maximum of the premium sold and risk owning the stock at lower valuation. The covered combination lets us take advantage of higher implied volatility readings, participate in appreciation to the call's strike price, but risk owning double the position at a lower valuation. We might consider using this strategy by purchasing between a quarter and a half position and selling an equivalent number of calls and puts.

Here's how the numbers might work using quarter size positions.

Strategy 1: Buy the stock. Buy a position (here a quarter position) in XYZ at $39.17. Maximum upside is unlimited; maximum risk is $39.17. The break-even point is $39.17.

Strategy 2: Write a put. Sell a quarter position in XYZ for $5.10, with two months to expiration and a strike price of $30. If the stock holds above the $30 strike until expiration, the maximum profit is $5.10 per share, or 127.6 percent, based on the industry minimum capital requirement. If the stock drops and the put is assigned, the cost of owning the shares is $24.90, or 36.4 percent below the current stock price. The downside break-even point is $24.90.

Strategy 3: Covered combination. Buy a quarter position and sell an equivalent number of calls with a $50 strike for $4.50 and puts with a $30 strike for $5.10, both with two months until expiration. If the stock is called at $50, maximum profit is $20.24 per share, or 106.5 percent. If the stock remains at $39.17 and the options depreciate, the profit is $9.41 per share, or 49.5 percent. If the stock declines and the put is assigned, the manager owns a half position at an average price of $29.88 per share, or 23.7 percent below the stock's current price. (This assumes 5 percent margin interest and no dividends or transaction charges.)

As the strategies show, the covered combination and the put write offer the highest premium levels, and therefore greater chance of success. The covered combination's maximum upside participation occurs at the $50 strike and is 27.6 percent for a potential profit of 106.5 percent. (This is an extreme, but could follow a sharp correction.) The put's maximum potential gain (from premium capture) is $5.10 per share, or 127.6 percent.

At the beginning of a new bull market, many managers and investors may not feel confident about the market's new direction. They may miss the initial movement as well as some substantial gains by believing that stocks cannot rise while the economy is weak or declining. Yet despite the negative press and earnings reports, share prices are headed up. This may occur when volatility and fear levels are high.

A new bull market is often heralded by improving internal market indicators, such as the advance-decline indicators, rising volume compared with declining volume, and other internal market indicators. Markets set a declining number of new lows. Stocks and sectors rise above their 50-day moving averages, and those averages begin to slope upward. Implied volatility, as measured by the CBOE S&P 500 Implied Volatility Index (VIX) and other volatility indicators, drops to about half of its range for the past 52 weeks. All these are lagging indicators.

It's sometimes possible to find early indicators, too. A change in commodities, currencies, debt, real estate, or other investment vehicles may presage a change in equities. A noteworthy event—even one that doesn't appear to be associated with stocks or the economy—may turn things around. It's unwise to declare market bottoms or tops while events are in progress, but managers who pay attention can sometimes get clues about which way the markets are heading.

Once a market trend gets established, other indicators fall into line. In most cases a positive intermediate-term trend of more than two months emerges, volume returns, and the advance broadens. The number of new lows wanes; the number of new highs begins to expand. More companies trade above their 50-day, and eventually 200-day, moving averages. Higher lows, and eventually higher highs, help further the positive trend. Sector leadership—sometimes from a surprising sector—emerges, implied volatility numbers decline, and the volatility skew improves.

The percentage of NYSE stocks trading above their 200-day moving averages indicates a rally's strength. A rising number is always good. A reading above 50 percent is positive, signaling that more than half the issues on the "Big Board" are positive. A reading near 90 percent suggests that the rally may be overextended. Managers should look for groups or issues that may be overbought or near correction.

The recovery rally that followed the 2007–2009 bear market showed extremely strong stocks. By Labor Day the major benchmarks were up more than 50 percent from their respective lows. Nearly 91 percent of NYSE stocks traded above their 200-day moving averages, an extremely high reading and a rise from very poor February lows. TRADPAUS, the Bloomberg ticker for the percentage of stocks trading above their 200-day moving averages, rose from 1 percent to 91 percent in less than six months (Figure 16.1).

Consider another example. After setting a nearly seven-year low on an almost 50 percent retracement during a bear market, the price of natural gas begins to rise. Shares of companies related to natural gas start to break out, a group that includes Penn Virginia Corp. (PVA—$22.90), which formed a short-term, inverse head-and-shoulders reversal pattern on the weekly chart and broke out from a four-month base.

PVA is a small-cap company and was rising in line with or slightly behind its larger peers. Market analysts expected a modest rise toward $36, where the 100-week and 200-week moving averages converge. Charts showed strong resistance near $38 (Figure 16.2); the stock had already passed resistance near $30 and $32.80.

Despite the 10-month drop in share price, implied and historical volatility levels had just set a new 52-week low (Figure 16.3). The at-the-money

Figure 16.1 Percentage of stocks on the New York Stock Exchange trading above their respective 200-day moving averages.

Figure 16.2 A weekly chart on Penn Virginia Corp. (PVA). Note that the stock has broken the 14-month negative resistance trend line and is breaking out from a four-month base and inverse head-and-shoulders reversal pattern. The dotted lines show resistance, with the line weight indicating the resistance's significance.

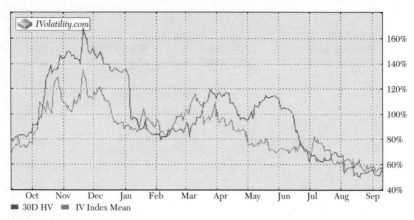

Figure 16.3 Implied and historic volatility chart on Penn Virginia Corp. (PVA), courtesy of iVolatility.com.

skew showed that implied volatility was lower over the two front-most months before rising. The implied volatility index, as published by iVolatility.com, was 57.60 percent on September 3.

I had two trading suggestions for a client who wanted to take a position without buying stock. The first was to purchase a six-week call that was just in the money, which had a $22.50 strike price and cost $1.75. I suggested an initial option target of $4.50 and a stop at $1.15. The maximum profit potential was unlimited, maximum risk was $1.75, and the break-even point was the stock at $24.25 at expiration.

A second idea was to sell six-week put contracts with a $20 strike for $1.30. If the stock remained above the $20 strike price and the put expired, the client would see a profit of $1.30 (premium capture) and a return of 56.8 percent, based on the industry minimum margin requirement. If the shares dropped below the $20 strike and the put were exercised, the fund would own the shares at an effective price of $18.70 per share, or 18.3 percent below then-current market value.

Investors who thought the shares might break above the resistance at $38 might buy a six-month call (the longest then available) with a $20 strike for $3.90. This option puts the would-be buyer in a long position, but with capital risk that's approximately 83 percent lower than the capital risk of buying stock. The option is in-the-money, so it has a positive delta of 70 percent, meaning that the option will rise or fall 70 cents for the next

1-point move, up or down, in the underlying stock. This strategy may fit fund needs while also reducing risk.

Instead of buying stock, consider purchasing an equivalent number of calls and investing the difference in low-risk Treasury bonds. If the stock price rises above $36 after a month or two, write some out-of-the-money calls, such as those with a $40 strike, against the purchased long calls, to reduce risk and help the portfolio benefit from the passage of time. Or swap the call with a $20 strike into one with a $30 or $35 strike, selling a portion of the position to remove capital risk or take profits. Remember that seasonal factors could affect the shares as winter progresses.

The Trading Market

Investors buy and hold for the long term. Traders, by contrast, buy and sell faster and more often, taking advantage of shorter-term trends to turn a profit. Traders can nearly always find things and ways to trade—sometimes more easily, sometimes with more difficulty. Countertrend, nested movements provide traders with shorter-term opportunities in a long-term investment market.

Sometimes a market's primary trend favors investors. Sideways and bear markets are usually trading markets, because most investors cannot succeed in longer sideways markets, which lack momentum, or through major downward trends. Downward trends are often volatile, and traders can frequently turn volatility to their favor. The relationship between SPX and the implied volatility on its options is illustrated on the weekly chart, shown on Figure 16.4.

Traders can also profit by using short-term and intermediate-term oscillators in a trading market. Selling calls on overbought issues or selling puts on oversold issues may provide alternatives to selling or buying shares, especially when premiums are elevated. When using short-term options, traders can also benefit from option premium decay when trends turn sideways or a reversal lacks momentum, lowering the time risk as well. If the stock doesn't change direction, a trader may buy an offsetting hedge or sell an opposing option to contain risk. (Stops or real hedges are even better ways to control risk.)

Let's look at an example of a stock in a trading environment. Figure 16.5 is a weekly chart on Kraft Foods (KFT—$28.10). The stock has been choppy since rising from its lows in February 2009. The intermediate-term

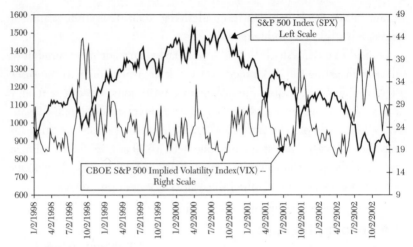

Figure 16.4 A weekly chart of the S&P 500 Index (SPX) and the CBOE S&P 500 Implied Volatility Index (VIX) from 1998–2002. Note how volatility tends to accelerate when the market is declining.

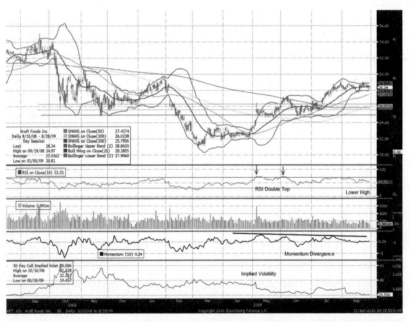

Figure 16.5 Daily chart on Kraft Foods (KFT) from the Bloomberg Professional Service Launchpad. Note the lower high in the RSI that followed the double top, the momentum divergence, and the low implied volatility readings.

trend has been positive, but the stock has failed to set a meaningful higher high. The long-term trend remains negative.

At the time, KFT was testing against the upper Bollinger Band line, an indication that it was overbought. Additionally, the Relative Strength Index (RSI) was overbought, with a previous double top that tested the previous September's highs, then moved quickly into a major decline. The momentum gauge shows a divergence with a lower high.

KFT's implied volatility had dropped to a low level. KFT is a consumer staples company and generally has below-average implied volatility levels, because it is considered a defensive stock.

Traders could take advantage of a potential correction by purchasing a put or bear spread using puts. Investors might purchase the put or spread as a hedge against the short-term action. If the stock moves higher before correcting, the increase would reduce the upside potential by just the hedge cost—not limited by a call contract's strike price.

As expected, the stock turned rather sharply lower, breaking the consolidation support with a negative gap. The negative gap was not anticipated; it brought on a drop of roughly 10 percent from the recent highs.

Instead of trading on overbought or oversold readings, some traders wait for stronger, timelier, confirmed signals, such as those offered by stochastic oscillators or the RSI. Sometimes, however, this strategy means missing an opportunity when the stock moves suddenly. Consider watching for subtle changes, which may involve zooming in on the chart for a more detailed view. The RSI's signals confirm when the indicator changes direction and crosses above 30 percent. The stochastic oscillator's signal occurs when %K crosses %D.

Momentum changes may offer another early warning. While shares rise, the momentum indicators may wane, or volume may drop off. This is a sign that demand (in an uptrend) or supply (in a downtrend) may be nearing exhaustion, or that a countertrend movement is in the offing. In a rising trend with diminishing momentum, it may be more appropriate to write an out-of-the-money call, because shares may enter a consolidation or very minor correction instead of a decline. This is especially likely if the stock has been a market or sector leader and a correction is at hand. Check relative performance.

Trading around a position can contribute to alpha, especially when volatility increases. Purchasing a put against a long position may offer benefits no matter which way the market moves, especially if gamma increases. These changes may pump additional premium into a contract, adding to the position's value. Note, however, that it may be very difficult to offset a share's position loss if you buy one contract for each 100 shares, at least in the short term.

Many traders also buy pairs trades: in this case, two stocks (or a stock and an exchange-traded fund) moving in the same direction, generally in the same sector. One of the pair (the leader) moves ahead of the other (the follower). A trader may identify overbought stocks or those nearing resistance and take a negative position on that issue and a positive position in the lagging shares. The leading stock will likely become overbought before the lagging stock, so traders try to take advantage of both valuations. And because both are in the same sector, one position would likely offset a strong movement from the other, lowering overall risk. (This is generally not the case for special situation companies, such as acquisition targets or those that anticipate significant news.)

Traders use puts and calls to increase their returns, creating alpha while lowering or changing their risk exposure. Consider some examples.

In March 2009, retailers' shares were very strong, as the market began its recovery from one of the worst bear markets in 40 years. This is a bit odd, as discretionary spending tends to lag improvements in economic conditions and consumer confidence. Shares of electronics seller Best Buy (BBY) rose sharply and outperformed the broad market and the group for nearly a month (Figure 16.6.) The relative performance section shows BBY's performance versus the SPDR S&P Retail ETF. The stock then entered a consolidation with some corrective action. The highs set on April 22 were tested months later, but remained the stock's significant resistance. Even as the group rose, BBY shares stayed put.

Unusually, relative performance and the RSI peaked at nearly the same time. (In most situations, managers should look for divergences.) The stock continued to move higher but momentum had already rolled off its peak, an indication that the advance was losing steam.

XRT and BBY began to move higher around the same time. XRT continued to rise after BBY peaked, and the shares reached overbought levels in May. Following a short correction, XRT moved to a marginally

Crucial

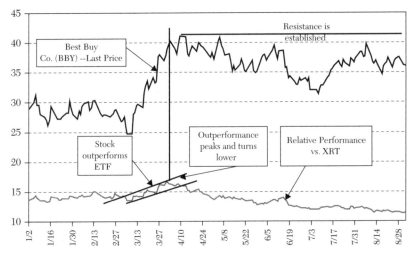

Figure 16.6 Daily chart on Best Buy Co. (BBY) and relative performance vs. the SPDR S&P Retail ETF (XRT). Notice how the shares peak just after relative performance. The RSI oscillator was overbought, and the stock stalled and moved sideways before turning lower.

higher high. A pause in the advance produced a higher low, which ultimately led to a positive breakout in July. Based on other retailers' upward movement, a pairs trade was potentially a good strategy.

On April 9 the BBY May 42-1/2 calls traded around $2; XRT May 26 calls were $1.35. Purchase the XRT calls and write the BBY calls for a net credit of $0.65 per share, or $65.00 per option. Ideally, the electronics retailer corrects or stays the same, and the group continues appreciating.

XRT continued to rise until an overbought correction began on May 6. An astute trader would have likely closed the position on May 8, following XRT's worst one-day performance in months. At that point XRT was $27.32 and May 26 calls cost $1.60. BBY May 42-1/2 calls cost around $0.05. Traders who closed the position would collect a credit of $1.65 and added that to the original credit of $0.65, for a total profit of $2.30 per share.

If the group had turned sharply lower, a trader would have realized a maximum profit of $0.65 per share when both contracts expired worthless. If the sector had rallied sharply with BBY outperformance, traders may have lost money, depending on the degree of outperformance, the call's liability, and the profit that they realized from a long call purchased on XRT. BBY might have been acquired, or some other factor could have sharply disengaged the stock from the group. Events like these are unlikely but possible, so managers should be wary.

This pairs trade would work particularly well for a manager who is long BBY stock, with an unrealized gain, letting that manager trade around a position and take advantage of the stock's overbought status and changing relative performance relationship.

It's important to monitor pair trades and other trading strategies, as they can be much more sensitive than investment strategies. Check execution costs, margin requirements, and interest costs, which may significantly reduce a strategy's value. Finally, make sure your fund is allowed to take on a particular transaction. Some funds have mandates that do not allow them to trade on a short-term basis or take offsetting positions.

Japanese Candlesticks

Japanese candlestick charts compare opening and closing values for a stated period. The candle body is the difference between those values; the shadows measure between the highs, the lows, and the candle body, combining to tell the story of trading for the period. A white candle body indicates that the closing value was higher than the opening value; a dark candle shows that the last price was below the opening value.

Very short-term traders, such as market makers, floor traders, or day traders, may look to intraday charts for signals that help them move in and out of positions, often making very limited profits. Potentially limited gains plus limited times can make trading options around these positions difficult, but traders—especially options market makers—may use these signals to help them balance their holdings.

Reversal signals don't always indicate reversal actions. A Japanese reversal signal sometimes indicates that a trend has halted and that a sideways trend may take its place, instead of a countertrend movement. Reversal signals, like any other pattern, can fail—or another reversal signal may follow them. These signals are stronger when they're combined with other, similar signals from an oscillator or other technical gauge.

Signals generated on longer-term charts take longer to build, and so they are more significant than those generated on shorter-term graphs.

Figure 16.7 is a weekly graph of Massey Energy Co. (MEE). The last candle on this chart, from July 4, shows a negative engulfing and penetrating candle that ended a 14-week positive trend channel. The stock had been overbought, according to the RSI oscillator, for most of that trend. Momentum and relative performance peaked just ahead of the negative candle.

Implied volatility levels were near 81 percent when the signal occurred. Given that the signal was on a weekly chart, the impact had greater significance than a similar signal on a daily chart. Traders may have purchased a bear ratio spread, buying the July 75 puts and selling the July 65 puts for a $2.40 net debit on a 1-by-2 basis. If the stock dropped to $65, or 13.3 percent below current share value, traders might have realized the maximum potential profit of $7.60 per share. Below that level, the profit would have eroded on a point-for-point basis, due to the naked put.

As it happened, the stock closed at $67.01 two weeks later, at July expiration. This gave traders a profit of $5.60 per share. Following a two-week pause, the stock resumed its downward move.

Figure 16.7 Weekly chart on Massey Energy Co. (MEE) showing negative engulfing/penetrating candle. This reversal pattern ended a 14-week positive trend channel.

Funds that were long the stock before the reversal could also have moved to reduce risk and create alpha. A longer time frame might have worked well, perhaps including a collar strategy using August options. With the stock's high near $93 near the week's beginning and shares now at $75, managers might have sold the August 90 calls at $3.80 and purchased the August 65 puts at $3.70 for a $0.10 net credit. This move also means agreeing to sell the stock at an effective price of $90.10 if it went back to test the highs, or to sell shares at an effective price of $65.10 if the negative trend continued.

Stock shares cost $60.40 at expiration. Following a short bounce, shares turned lower again and fell into the teens by November. Our hypothetical fund would have sold the shares at $65, protecting the position by limiting exposure. With the original share purchase near $40, the fund realized a gain.

Other Investment and Trading Opportunities

Special events, such as mergers and takeovers, new product releases, or other news items, as well as market events, such as expiration's approach, offer opportunities to both traders and investors.

A phenomenon called "pinning" occurs during expiration week and is based on a particular option's gravitational pull. When market makers, traders, arbitragers, institutional fund managers, and even retail investors are interested in at-the-money or near-the-money puts and calls, the ways they adjust their positions can lead share price. The higher the open interest level, which shows the number of outstanding contracts, the greater the probability that pinning will take place.

The list of potential pinning stocks changes on a daily basis, based on movements in the market, stocks, volatility, and options. I usually look at pinning candidates starting on Tuesday morning of expiration week.

Options professionals try to close unhedged positions toward the middle of expiration week. This generally lets them adjust risk and benefit from time decay on previously sold contracts. In many instances they roll positions to the next expiration month, reestablishing time decay. Some positions roll diagonally, changing both expiration month and strike price in response to a change in volatility or in the underlying stock price. If the contract lacks liquidity, with no one to take the other side of a trade, a manager may hold a short option until expiration. If that option is in the money at expiration, the option will likely be exercised and the writer will have to purchase (put) or sell (call) the shares.

Considering stocks with high option interest at a concentrated strike price lets us take a position that would benefit from a gravitational move toward that price. If the strike is above the current stock price we would hope for a move up, and so we would buy a bull spread with a call at a low strike and sell a call with the target strike price. If the strike price is below the stock's current price we would hope for a drop, so we would purchase an in-the-money put with a higher strike price and sell a put with the target strike price.

We might also sell the straddle (put and call together) on that strike price. This can be profitable if the options are not prematurely assigned. To make the practice worthwhile, make sure that the contracts have some time premium. I have seen traders write either option or straddle and then be caught, especially when the company became an acquisition target. Additionally, watch for stocks going ex-dividend or reporting earnings in the near future.

Investment funds with long stock positions can also use pinning to their advantage. Consider writing out-of-the-money calls against stock shares when the stock is above the pinning strike price. Go out another month from the upcoming expiration to collect some premium. If the distance between the stock price and the pinning strike price is relatively small, a manager may consider taking no action, because the decline may not erode the price of the option written during that short period of time.

Managers who want to add to or initiate a position could write a put with the pinning strike price but with an extra month until expiration, or enter an order to buy the stock near the strike price. Enter the order just above the strike. Managers tend to find buy and sell orders when the price of the underlying shares is equivalent to the strike, which could mean missing the trade. The pinning's timing combined with potential movement can create alpha without the need to use options or take an immediate position.

Upcoming Events

Expected or not, company events—a new or redesigned product or service, a new drug or device approval—can move a stock. Once again, traders and some investors can take advantage of the situation.

Traders may purchase straddles or strangles before an expected announcement—sometimes weeks ahead, to benefit from a possibly early announcement or from stock moves ahead of a release date. Whether a stock rises sharply on good news or falls dramatically on bad, trading both expectations helps traders gain either way. This practice is known as "buying gamma," or volatility.

In September 2009, health care watchers awaited data from Arena Pharmaceuticals (ARNA) on a new obesity drug, lorcaserin. The stock had risen from April lows and was now trading above $5. Since the end of July implied volatility levels had shot up more than threefold, from a low near 70 percent to more than 246 percent (Figure 16.8). Implied volatility set a new 52-week high while the stock was well below its 52-week high of $7.42 and above its 52-week low of $2.26. Expectations were running very high.

Then the markets heard that drug results were underwhelming, ahead of an FDA announcement, and that knocked the stock down more than 10 percent in one day. A strangle purchased in early August would have been more profitable than one bought closer to the announcement date.

Strangles and straddles let purchasers benefit from stock price fluctuations. Managers might sell calls when the stock is moving higher and sell puts when the stock is moving lower.

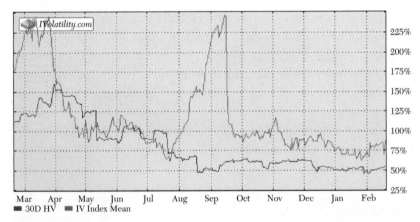

Figure 16.8 One-year daily chart of implied and historic volatility on Arena Pharmaceuticals (ARNA), courtesy of iVolatility.com.

Investors could benefit from the sharp rise in volatility, too. Purchasing the stock near its lows and writing out-of-the-money calls may provide some income, as well as a downside cushion if the drug is not approved. When the stock traded at $5, more than double its low, investors might have sold one-month October 6 calls at $1.20. Should the stock increase and the share be called away, the effective sale price would be $7.20, 44 percent above current market price. The premium could also offset risk and cost, giving a cost of about $1 per share if the stock was purchased near its low.

An investor who purchased shares near the lows and was concerned about drug trial outcomes could swap the stock position for an option position. With ARNA's implied volatility levels high, the holder could have sold the stock and the October 4 puts at $1.00. If shares fell below the $4 strike after the release, the shares would likely be repurchased for an effective cost of $3.00 per share, or about 40 percent below the price when the trade was initiated. If the stock rallied on a favorable release, the investor would capture the $1 premium, which is 20 percent of the stock price.

Mergers and Acquisitions

Any merger or acquisition announcement, regardless of its fine print, often pushes options premiums sharply higher. Premiums then typically contract significantly, especially if no rival bidders are anticipated and there are no expectations that the deal will be blocked. In most cases the target company will trade in a narrowing sideways pattern, if the arrangement is a cash transaction, or will take on the acquiring company's characteristics in a stock transaction.

In a merger paid for through a stock swap, traders may benefit by purchasing the acquiring company and selling the company being acquired, if there is an economic difference between the two values. This creates arbitrage. Sometimes managers create options arbitrage strategies and pair them against each other. As the deal reaches maturity, price discrepancies will disappear.

A fund manager might hold shares in a targeted acquisition and try to maintain the position, but swap the stock for that of the acquiring company. To do this, initiate a trade that is similar to a reverse conversion: Sell the long shares, buy a call, and sell a put in the same series. This creates a synthetic long position, but removes the stock from the equation.

When a fund is short the acquiring company, its manager can repurchase the shares, then sell a call and purchase a put in the same series, creating a synthetic short sale. This trade may be a good choice when there is a shortage of stock to be loaned, or when rebate fees are expected to jump sharply.

CHAPTER 17

All About
Resources

I HOPE THIS BOOK WILL give you a deeper understanding of technical analysis and options strategies. No matter how well you understand them, however, you'll need solid information from good sources to move your strategies from theory to reality.

Abundance of Resources

There are a number of information services from which you might choose. Many of these information sources are very good, but no matter which you choose, it is very difficult to get by with just one. Vendors often have their own specialties, so you may choose several.

Information quality is one of the most important reasons for choosing a vendor. Other good reasons include cost, ease of use, technology, support, data integrity, and functionality. The information you pay for should add insight and substance while saving time.

Choose both long- and short-term data that you can trust to build reliable charts. Technical analysis uses graphs as a basis for making decisions, and garbage data create useless graphs. Vendors play a key role in keeping data clean, and some vendors handle this better than others. Check your vendor before trusting the charts.

Bloomberg Professional Service

Many managers use the Bloomberg Professional Service (BPS) for quotes, information, and charts. Over the years, I have seen tremendous improvement in BPS charts. They let the user select different time frames with data going back several decades. Data integrity appears to be high. Charts on BPS's main site let you draw trend lines and add a limited number of indicators.

Figure 17.1 shows a BPS intraday graph on Verizon Communications (VZ). I have added a 13-tick moving average and a trend line.

Figure 17.2 is a daily VZ chart with an added relative strength index (RSI) oscillator. The chart is easily accessible from other screens (Figure 17.3). Users can manipulate time frames, add analytical tools, draw trend lines, and zoom in or out in order to get a more detailed view—all useful features. However, the chart's readability is not as good as that of some others, including another BPS Launchpad chart package.

Figure 17.4 is more dynamic. Based on the BPS Launchpad, it offers many of the same features as previous charts, plus some additional analytical and drawing abilities. This chart can expand or contract to fit a workstation desktop; it updates itself dynamically, including studies and other features. The user can change background and foreground colors, making for easier readability and

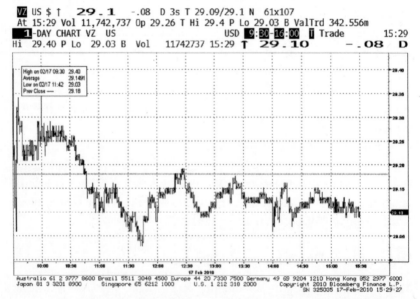

Figure 17.1 Intraday chart on Verizon Communications (VZ) from the main monitor screen on the Bloomberg Professional Service.

Figure 17.2 Daily candlestick chart on Verizon Communications (VZ) from the main monitor screen on the Bloomberg Professional Service. Note the RSI on the screen and the added function buttons above the chart.

Page   Equity**DES**
Hit 1 <GO> for more balance sheet information (CH3).
BALANCE SHEET   (Mil of USD)   Page 9 /10
VZ US   VERIZON COMMUNICATIONS INC

	12/2009	12/2008		12/2009	12/2008
Cash & Near Cash	2009.00	9782.00	Accounts Payable	15223.00	13814.00
Marketable sec	490.00	509.00	ST borrowings	7205.00	4993.00
Accounts & Notes R	12573.00	11703.00	Other ST liab	6708.00	7099.00
Inventories	2289.00	2092.00	Current Liabilitie	29136.00	25906.00
Other Current Asse	5247.00	1989.00			
Current Assets	22608.00	26075.00	LT Debt	55051.00	46959.00
			Other LT Liabiliti	58697.00	50582.00
LT Investments & L		4781.00	Noncur liabilities	113748.00	97541.00
			Total Liabilities	142884.00	123447.00
Depr fixed assets	228518.00	213511.00			
Non-depr fixed ass		2094.00	Preferred Equity	.00	.00
Accumulated Deprec	137052.00	129059.00	Minority Interest	42761.00	37199.00
Net fixed assets	91466.00	86546.00	Share cap & APIC	40405.00	40588.00
			Retained earnings	1201.00	1118.00
Other Assets	113177.00	84950.00	Shareholders Equit	84367.00	78905.00
			Tot liab & equity	227251.00	202352.00
Total Assets	227251.00	202352.00			
			ST part of LT debt	7205.00	4993.00
Shares Outstanding	2836.00	2840.52	# treasury shares		127.09
			Amt treasury stock	5000.00	4839.00

Australia 61 2 9777 8600 Brazil 5511 3048 4500 Europe 44 20 7330 7500 Germany 49 69 9204 1210 Hong Kong 852 2977 6000
Japan 81 3 3201 8900   Singapore 65 6212 1000   U.S. 1 212 318 2000   Copyright 2010 Bloomberg Finance L.P.
SN 325035 17-Feb-2010 15:28:09

Figure 17.3 A balance sheet on Verizon Communications (VZ) from the main monitor screen on the Bloomberg Professional Service. Enter the "GPC <GO>" command to move between this screen and the daily candlestick chart, shown in Figure 17.2, without entering the stock symbol again.

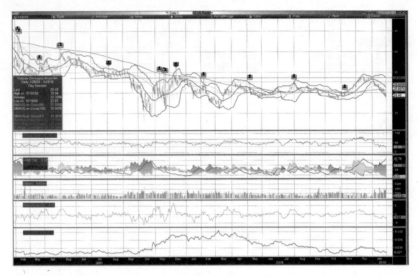

Figure 17.4 Another view of the daily chart on Verizon Communications (VZ) using the charting package on the Bloomberg Professional Services Launchpad.

an appealing visual presentation. (Notice the difference in resolution between Figures 17.4 and 17.2.) The Launchpad version offers greater clarity, flexibility, and functionality. A user can set alerts on the newer charts, monitoring activity but not watching every move an individual security makes.

The charting package also lets managers track events in the life of a stock, including quarterly earnings report releases, dividend payments, and shares traded by insiders. All these can help a manager decide to purchase, hold, or sell shares.

MetaStock Professional Service

MetaStock Professional Service offers sharp, crisp charts. Their data are fairly reliable—particularly the live feeds from Thomson Reuters—but delays may sometimes mean that a chart is not up-to-date. Graphic features and the copy and paste function are both good, as is the ability to create small chart books and set up templates, which can save a great deal of time. This system lets you save analytics and studies for particular securities and create your own customized studies, a growing trend. Users can change time periods (daily/weekly/monthly) at the click of a button and use toolbars to add lines, studies, and graphics.

SuperCharts, Worden Brothers, and Others

Other charting services, such as SuperCharts and Worden Brothers, are popular among industry professionals. These programs include many of their competitors' features.

Many other resources are available through the Internet. See a list of online options in Appendix A.

Chart Books

Chart books are also useful tools. They let managers look at a universe of stocks, flipping quickly through pages in search of eye-catching charts. These books are the most time-efficient way to regularly review many charts.

My company, Fullman Technologies, publishes several chart books each week, with offerings including daily, weekly, and monthly charts. One set of books focuses on particularly liquid stocks, with breakdowns by capitalization and sector (and a supplied scoring sheet). Another set uses the options universe as its basis; still another looks at a combination of U.S.-based, listed stocks and NASDAQ securities, both organized by sector. These books, appropriately titled *Fullman Technical Pictures*, also include information on the major market benchmarks, popular exchange-traded funds, currencies, commodities, economic data, and some leading international indices. Fullman also offers books with some proprietary analytical data, upcoming earnings reports, and economics calendars.

Available as PDF files, these books provide a timely product at a low cost. Most pages have eight charts, a manageable number for scanning or printing. Figure 17.5 shows a sample page of Fullman's weekly charts on high-cap energy stocks. Other companies, such as *Investor's Business Daily*, also publish chart books. See Appendix A for more information.

Scanning Techniques

Scanning techniques can help managers look at technical data without reading thousands of charts. Many technical services offer managers tools that help them scan a universe of stocks and either rank or highlight information that meets specified criteria. This lets managers quickly pick out stocks of interest.

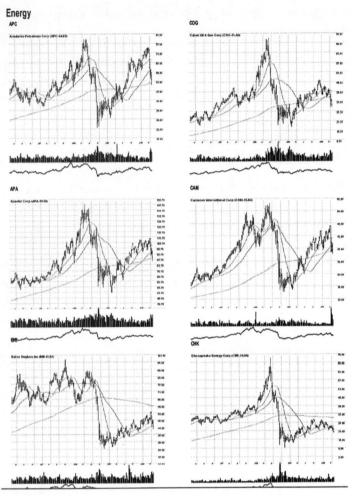

Figure 17.5 A page from the Fullman Technical Pictures weekly chart book showing high-cap energy stocks.

BPS lets users customize scans to include fundamental data, such as price/earnings ratios, PEG, market capitalization, and a host of other variables. Users can create their own criteria by using a screen within the function, then save the form and its variables to use as often as they like. This is a very useful way to filter fundamental and technical data and to search for companies based on their corporate profiles. Figure 17.6 shows part of a BPS filtering screen's output.

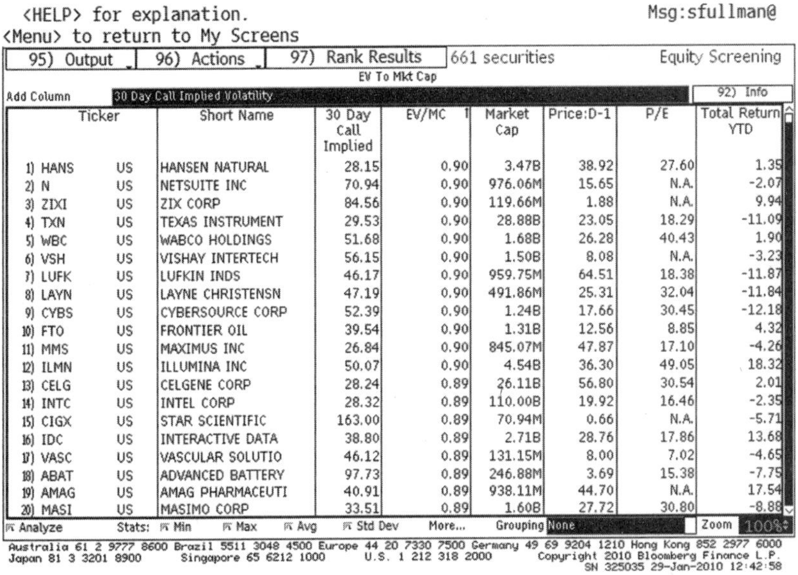

<HELP> for explanation.   Msg:sfullman@
<Menu> to return to My Screens

| 95) Output | 96) Actions | 97) Rank Results | 661 securities | | | Equity Screening |

EV To Mkt Cap

Add Column | 30 Day Call Implied Volatility | | | | | | | 92) Info |

Ticker		Short Name	30 Day Call Implied	EV/MC	Market Cap	Price:D-1	P/E	Total Return YTD
1) HANS	US	HANSEN NATURAL	28.15	0.90	3.47B	38.92	27.60	1.35
2) N	US	NETSUITE INC	70.94	0.90	976.06M	15.65	N.A.	-2.07
3) ZIXI	US	ZIX CORP	84.56	0.90	119.66M	1.88	N.A.	9.94
4) TXN	US	TEXAS INSTRUMENT	29.53	0.90	28.88B	23.05	18.29	-11.09
5) WBC	US	WABCO HOLDINGS	51.68	0.90	1.68B	26.28	40.43	1.90
6) VSH	US	VISHAY INTERTECH	56.15	0.90	1.50B	8.08	N.A.	-3.23
7) LUFK	US	LUFKIN INDS	46.17	0.90	959.75M	64.51	18.38	-11.87
8) LAYN	US	LAYNE CHRISTENSN	47.19	0.90	491.86M	25.31	32.04	-11.84
9) CYBS	US	CYBERSOURCE CORP	52.39	0.90	1.24B	17.66	30.45	-12.18
10) FTO	US	FRONTIER OIL	39.54	0.90	1.31B	12.56	8.85	4.32
11) MMS	US	MAXIMUS INC	26.84	0.90	845.07M	47.87	17.10	-4.26
12) ILMN	US	ILLUMINA INC	50.07	0.90	4.54B	36.30	49.05	18.32
13) CELG	US	CELGENE CORP	28.24	0.89	26.11B	56.80	30.54	2.01
14) INTC	US	INTEL CORP	28.32	0.89	110.00B	19.92	16.46	-2.35
15) CIGX	US	STAR SCIENTIFIC	163.00	0.89	70.94M	0.66	N.A.	-5.71
16) IDC	US	INTERACTIVE DATA	38.80	0.89	2.71B	28.76	17.86	13.68
17) VASC	US	VASCULAR SOLUTIO	46.12	0.89	131.15M	8.00	7.02	-4.65
18) ABAT	US	ADVANCED BATTERY	97.73	0.89	246.88M	3.69	15.38	-7.75
19) AMAG	US	AMAG PHARMACEUTI	40.91	0.89	938.11M	44.70	N.A.	17.54
20) MASI	US	MASIMO CORP	33.51	0.89	1.60B	27.72	30.80	-8.88

P\ Analyze   Stats: P\ Min   P\ Max   P\ Avg   P\ Std Dev   More...   Grouping None   Zoom 100%

Australia 61 2 9777 8600 Brazil 5511 3048 4500 Europe 44 20 7330 7500 Germany 49 69 9204 1210 Hong Kong 852 2977 6000
Japan 81 3 3201 8900   Singapore 65 6212 1000   U.S. 1 212 318 2000   Copyright 2010 Bloomberg Finance L.P.
                                                                              SN 325035 29-Jan-2010 12:42:58

Figure 17.6 The equity screening function on the Bloomberg Professional Service.

Fullman Technologies also offers a screening service that looks at technical factors, including overbought and oversold readings, candlestick signals, and volume breakouts. Most of the information is about stocks in the options universe, and users can choose daily, weekly, or monthly analysis.

Many of my clients find the screening service helpful in managing portfolios, including writing calls against long stock positions when the relative strength index (RSI) or stochastic oscillators indicate overbought conditions. The screening process identifies the most significant candidates, cutting down the necessary time for making these decisions. I have also customized these programs to focus on just a fund's holdings, or to otherwise meet managers' requirements in ways that add value and improve time management. Figure 17.7 shows the output of a daily volume breakout on options stocks.

BPS uses the Option Block ticker function to let users see unusual options volume and sharp changes in implied volatility, which users can employ to catch movements in the underlying stock. This window shows option block trades. Managers can also look at individual options trading and see whether they traded on the offer or bid side of the market.

Technical Signals

Daily signals: new highs new lows strongest moneyflows weakest moneyflows stochastic buy signals stochastic sell signals rsi buy signals rsi sell signals
positive candlestick signals negative candlestick signals strongest performers weakest performers positive 10-day breakout negative 10-day breakout low adx report volume breakout strongest positive trends strongest negative trends
Weekly signals: stochastic buy signals stochastic sell signals rsi buy signals rsi sell signals
positive 5-week breakout negative 5-week breakout
Quantitative signals: Upcoming Dividend Payments

Volume Breakout Report

Company Name	Symbol	Last Price	Change	% Chg	Volume	Average Volume	% Average Difference
4KIDS ENTERTAINMENT INC	KDE	0.78	-0.08	-9.3	2,932	603	386.2
ABITIBI-CONSOLIDATED INC	ABY	2.26	-0.01	-0.4	65,570	29,024	125.9
ABRAXIS BIOSCIENCE INC	ABBI	21.47	-0.03	-0.1	5,664	3,439	64.7
ACCURIDE CORP	ACW	0.17	-0.20	-54.1	20,883	6,532	219.7
ACERGY SA-SPON ADR	ACGY	16.88	+1.13	+7.2	4,040	2,659	51.9
ADESA INC	KAR	27.82	...	...	15,755	5,951	164.7
ADVANTA CORP-CL B	ADVNB	0.04	-0.01	-20.0	15,867	9,598	65.3
AFFILIATED COMPUTER SVCS-A	ACS	59.64	-1.39	-2.3	54,939	14,048	291.1
AGCO CORP	AG	25.55	+1.25	+5.1	26,945	17,470	54.2
AGL RESOURCES INC	ATG	33.50	10.68	12.1	8,160	4,812	69.6
AIRSPAN NETWORKS INC	AIRN	0.08	...	...	9,311	2,146	333.9
ALADDIN KNOWLEDGE SYSTEMS	ALDN	11.49	+0.53	+4.8	8,438	2,106	300.7
ALCOA INC	AA	11.72	+0.61	+5.5	628,340	276,105	127.6
ALESCO FINANCIAL INC	AFN	0.67	+0.09	+15.5	5,242	3,333	57.3
ALLIED CAPITAL CORP	ALD	4.59	+0.03	+0.6	41,208	18,847	118.6
ALTUS PHARMACEUTICALS INC	ALTU	0.09	+0.04	+80.0	162,960	22,424	626.7
AMERICAN GREETINGS CORP-CL A	AM	21.54	-0.04	-0.2	7,195	3,545	103.0
ANDREW CORP	ANDW	15.04	+0.03	+0.2	163,830	35,181	365.7
ANSOFT CORP	ANSI	35.71	+0.01	+0.0	12,637	2,106	500.0
ANTHRACITE CAPITAL INC	AHR	0.24	-0.14	-36.8	107,910	26,767	303.1
APRIA HEALTHCARE GROUP INC	AHG	20.99	+7.00	+50.0	171,240	14,192	1,106.6
AQUILA INC	ILA	4.04	+0.10	+2.5	242,000	42,463	469.9
ASA LTD	ASA	27.31	-1.17	-4.1	1,117	605	84.6
ASPECT MEDICAL SYSTEMS INC	ASPM	12.27	+0.27	+2.3	4,544	1,458	211.7
ASPREVA PHARMACEUTICALS CORP	ASPV	0.01	...	...	1,050	72	1,358.3
ASYST TECHNOLOGIES INC	ASYT	0.05	-0.01	-16.7	145,410	43,862	231.5
ATHEROGENICS INC	AGIX	0.07	-0.01	-12.5	18,428	10,516	75.2
AUTHORIZE.NET HOLDINGS INC	ANET	23.19	-0.18	-0.8	7,199	3,657	96.9
AVENTINE RENEWABLE ENERGY	AVR	0.10	-0.02	-16.7	36,008	11,150	222.9
AXA -SPONS ADR	AXA	21.56	+0.09	+0.4	9,855	4,912	100.6
AXCELIS TECHNOLOGIES INC	ACLS	2.07	+0.09	+4.5	11,399	7,375	54.6

Figure 17.7 Daily volume breakout on options stocks.

BPS lets users check unusual options activity reports, which show stocks with unusual options volume, sharp increases in implied volatility, or both. At times this report has produced signals before news events, including acquisition announcements. Compare the data using BPS functions to see if trading was on the bid or offer side.

Fund managers can customize these reports to provide just the data they want to see. Figure 17.8 shows an unusual options activity report from Fullman Technologies; Figure 17.9 shows a breakdown of trading on an options contract on BPS.

Basic Materials							
Symbol	Last price	Total call Volume		Total Put Volume		Multiple of ADV	Put/call Ratio
		Yest,	Average	Yest,	Average		
ARG	61.35	4,615	45	7,033	12	205.3	1.54
TCK	33.97	5,525	1,401	3,709	5.75	3.9	0.67

Source YUB Capital Group, Inc.

Communications							
Symbol	Last price	Total call Volume		Total Put Volume		Multiple of ADV	Put/call Ratio
		Yest,	Average	Yest,	Average		
GLW	17.76	6,287	2,299	3,541	2,272	2.1	0.56
JDSU	8.15	7,292	1,112	431	656	4.4	0.06
NCK	13.35	17,582	9,274	33/094	2,219	4.8	2.17
SYLC	17.06	5,000	1,656	119	1,741	1.5	0.02

Source YUB Capital Group, Inc.

Consumer-Non-cyclical and Healthcare							
Symbol	Last price	Total call Volume		Total Put Volume		Multiple of ADV	Put/call Ratio
		Yest,	Average	Yest,	Average		
AET	28.97	14,732	2,194	7,916	1,030	2.1	0.53
AMT	55.76	9,409	3,049	224	744	2.5	0.02
GILD	46.30	23,342	3,740	2,705	2,425	4.2	0.12
HGSI	27.06	33,233	2,779	1,375	876	1.4	0.12
NCI	38.59	515	156	8,297	1,680	4.8	13.49
MA	223.45	5,777	1,450	4,525	1,242	3.8	0.78
PFE	17.88	20,340	25,571	17/639	5,417	1.2	0.97
SFD	15.38	7,480	377	170	624	7.7	0.02
Y"	83.27	7,357	3,605	8,073	1,660	2.9	1.10

Source YUB Capital Group, Inc.

Figure 17.8 The Unusual Options Activity Report from Fullman Technologies, Inc. This report may show unusual options volume, sharp increases in implied volatility, or both.

MSQ+BT US 2 C32.00 $ ↓   .O4 -.13 I P .04/.05 I 417x2483
At 12:38 Vol 26,846 Op .1 P Hi .11 O Lo .03 A Prev .17 OpInt 75,722

MSQ US 2 C32 Equ	98) Time Ranges	99) Actions		Page 1 Trade Summary Matrix
From	09:30 01/29/10	No participation set	Calculation	Bloomberg
To	12:39 01/29/10	No price or volume ranges set	Type	Volume
Interval Size	0.01	8) Set Limits	Format Net	Breakdown Bid/Mid/Ask

Calculation	VWAP	VWAP Volume	Std Deviation	Trades	Avg Trade Size
Bloomberg	0.0480	24,678	0.007707	310	80
Custom	0.0480	24,678	0.007707	310	80

Trades included in Bloomberg Calculation					
Price	Trades	Volume	Bid	Mid	Ask
0.11	1	25	0	0	25
0.10	2	45	0	0	45
0.09	1	1	0	0	1
0.08	3	66	0	0	66
0.07	10	363	0	103	260
0.06	40	2,637	1,199	564	874
0.05	190	12,837	1,916	872	10,049
0.04	61	8,647	8,103	72	472
0.03	2	57	57	0	0
Totals	310	24,678	11,275	1,611	11,792

1) Summary (VWAP) /\ 2) Top Trades (AQR) /\ 3) Price Chart (VAP) /\ 4) Price Table (TSM) /
Australia 61 2 9777 8600 Brazil 5511 3048 4500 Europe 44 20 7330 7500 Germany 49 69 9204 1210 Hong Kong 852 2977 6000
Japan 81 3 3201 8900   Singapore 65 6212 1000   U.S. 1 212 318 2000   Copyright 2010 Bloomberg Finance L.P.
SN 325035 29-Jan-2010 12:47:41

Figure 17.9 The Trade Summary Matrix (TSM) function on BPS shows the details of trading based on price and size on an options contract.

Options Resources

From simple to sophisticated, options traders and investors enjoy a host of available resources. As before, many professionals use more than one service, preferring one function, formula, or graphic treatment to another. Vendors have different strengths; some might be known for volatility analysis, others for strategy analytics.

Other Helpful Resources from Bloomberg

Bloomberg Professional Service offers many features connected to exchange-traded options. The options display screen—offered as part of the Launchpad or the options monitor (OMON) page—provides flexibility within a grid that has customized columns. I like the Launchpad screen better than the <OMON> page. Both have dynamic updating, but I find the stand-alone grid's look and feel more comfortable. Figure 17.10 shows the Launchpad screen.

Many other Bloomberg functions link to options screens. I find the top volume screen and the top trades screen (<TSM>) very useful. The Trade Summary Matrix function lets managers see whether a trade took place on the bid or offer side of the market and whether it traded alone, in conjunction with another option, or linked to a stock trade.

Bloomberg provides a position/risk screen, a volatility screen, and an implied and historic volatility screen (Figure 17.11, or <HIVG> on the Bloomberg monitor) that is extremely useful for comparing the price of the stock with volatility movements.

iVolatility

Many professionals consider iVolatility.com *the* authority on options. The service offers free or low-cost information on current implied volatility and historical volatility. Users can also buy downloads of historical data. The website shows the top and bottom five stocks with respect to volatility changes and makes comparisons between implied and historic volatility readings.

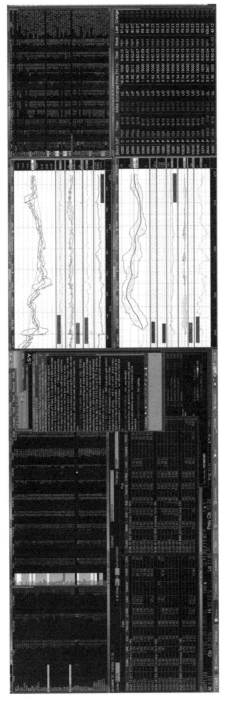

Figure 17.10 Bloomberg Professional Service Launchpad Options Monitor.

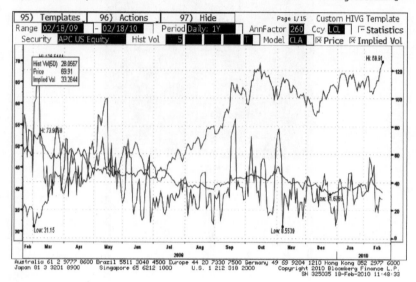

Figure 17.11 The Historic Implied Volatility screen from the Bloomberg Professional Service.

I built iVolatility.com's "The Strategist" features, which include some strategy scanners and worksheets for evaluating strategies. Figure 17.12a shows a strategist worksheet screen on a covered write; Figure 17.12b shows a strategist put-writing scanner.

Resources for Smaller Funds

Many funds have limited resources and can't afford high-end systems such as BPS. These funds have options, too. Quodd Financial Information Services offers quote and data services, including futures and options data, for a fraction of the cost of high-end services. The platform includes news services, such as Dow Jones, dynamic options data updating, and some high-end information, such as theoretical values, delta, gamma, theta, vega, and implied volatility calculations. These are also updated in real time. Figure 17.13 shows one of Quodd's several options screens.

I created some of Quodd's products, including *The Strategist Technical Pictures* chart books and some strategy scanners and worksheets. Quodd plans to offer a new graphics package and alert service in the near future.

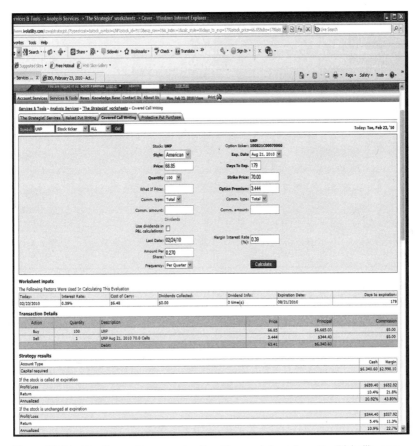

Figure 17.12a The Strategist covered call writing worksheet from the iVolatility.com website.

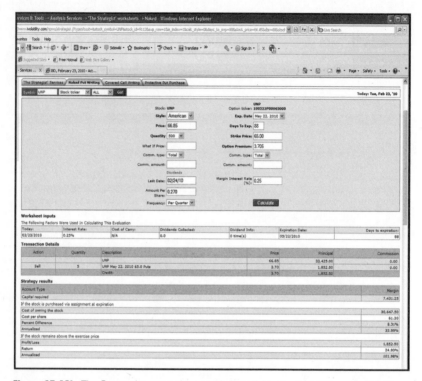

Figure 17.12b The Strategist put-writing worksheet from the iVolatility.com website.

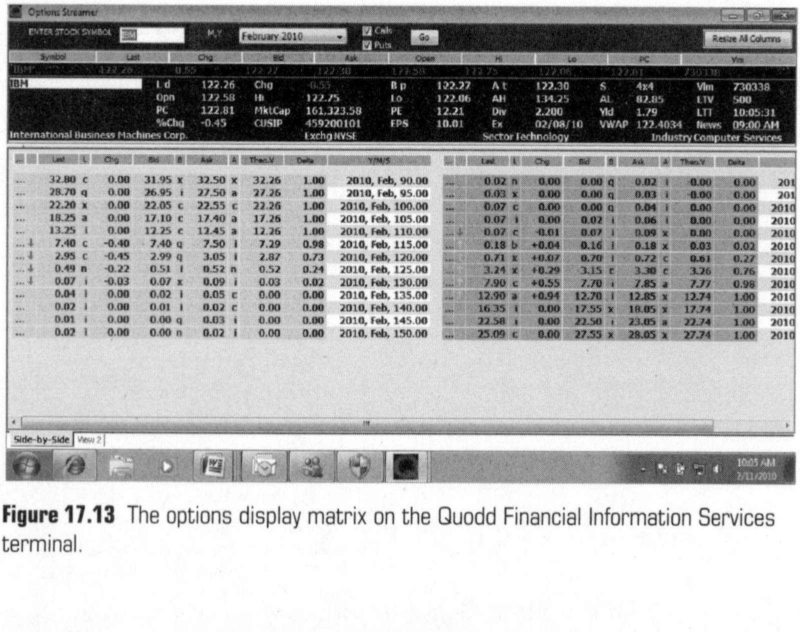

Figure 17.13 The options display matrix on the Quodd Financial Information Services terminal.

Analysts with limited budgets might also consider Track Data, a longtime mainstay of the options business. Still in business today, Track's offerings are supported by the company's option symbol database—one of the industry's best, and one that Track used to create analytical programs and drive models that professionals used for more than 30 years.

Risk and Position Monitoring

Large fund managers may have proprietary risk analysis systems; others may use third-party stand-alone applications or programs provided by a data vendor. Some managers develop their own spreadsheets, which allow them to monitor positions in either real time, delayed time, or end-of-trading time.

Those without such systems may like the Bloomberg Professional Service, which includes a function that lets users monitor portfolios and analyze scenarios. It also lets managers view strategies both numerically and graphically. The system has two major components. The first is the portfolio management function, PRTU <GO>, which lets users create a portfolio and add or remove stocks. The second portion is the options securities analysis program, reached by typing OSA<GO>.

The OSA screen lets users view positions with real-time updates and profit and loss data. It offers some risk analysis, including delta, gamma, and vega information for each position and in the aggregate. Figure 17.14 shows the screen. The positions in the sample portfolio include a covered combination on Dow Chemical (DOW), a naked put write on Chesapeake Energy (CHK), and a covered call writing position on Arch Coal (ACI).

BPS handles both simple and complex strategies. Figure 17.15 shows the scenario analysis in tabular format for the covered combination on DOW. The table shows an evaluation of aggregate stock positions, based on 1-point increments and the position's anticipated risk valuations. Change the date, and the system provides analytical data based on a change in days-to-expiration from the initial model. Changing the price is also a possibility.

Use the strategies tab to see the information in graphic form, based on a variation from the current price (x-axis) on different dates. See a profit/loss analysis and anticipated delta and gamma data.

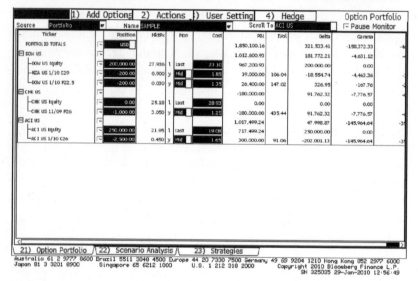

Figure 17.14 Bloomberg Professional Service—Options Securities Analysis (OSA) screen showing three strategies, including a covered combination, naked put, and covered call.

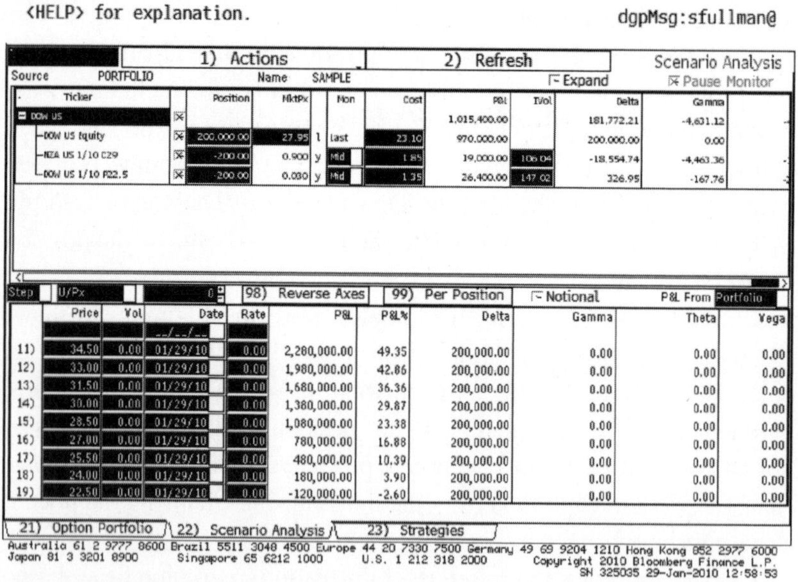

Figure 17.15 The OSA system on the Bloomberg Professional Service showing a tabular breakdown of anticipated profit/loss, as well as risk information on the covered combination of Dow Chemical (DOW).

Bloomberg offers other valuation and portfolio analysis screens, which users can employ to monitor positions, create strategy evaluations, or create a personal index. Bloomberg also provides cheat sheets to help users easily find functions.

iVolatility.com also offers a risk management product: a grid-based program that lets managers track their positions, profit and loss, volatility, and other option data. The system's quotes include risk valuations, as well as aggregate positions and their values, hypothetical scenarios, and stress testing. Figure 17.16 shows an iVolatility screen for Amgen Corp. (AMGN), along with options data and risk information.

Implied volatility values govern another live risk analysis system from iVolatility. The IVX Monitor grid, which comes in standard and customizable versions, can sit on a desktop or be embedded in a webpage. It shows changing implied volatility values and their respective 52-week

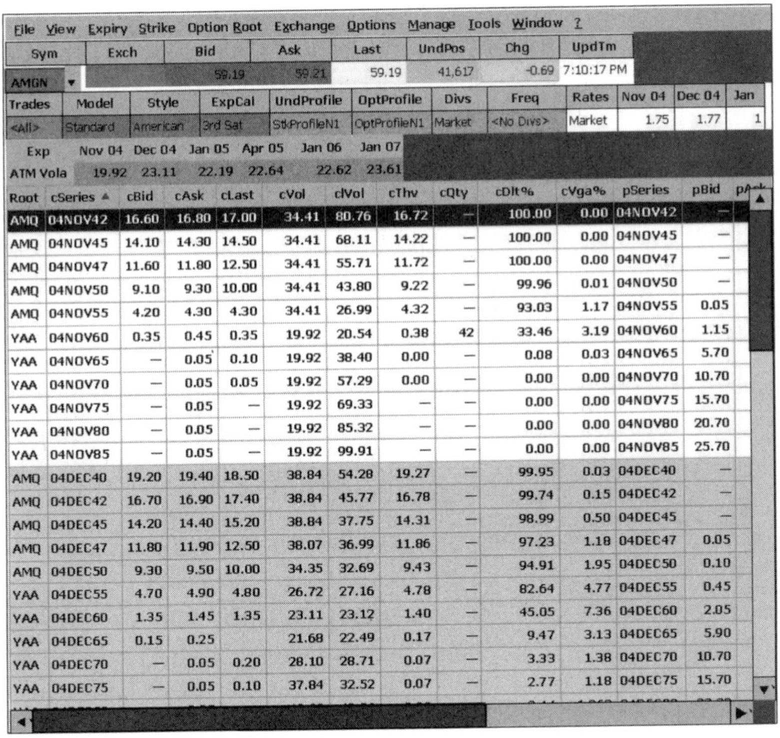

Figure 17.16 iVolatility.com's risk analysis system.

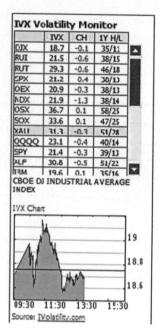

Figure 17.17 iVolatility.com IVX Gadget.

high and low values. Active traders and portfolio managers can benefit from having this information on their monitors. The monitor grid, shown as a computer gadget, is illustrated in Figure 17-17.

Different Funds, Different Vendors

Plenty of data vendors provide data, functionality, and insight. Managers have their own individual styles, guidelines, and objectives, so no one vendor is the right choice for every fund. Managers should acquaint themselves with the various product choices.

Each year the Securities Industry and Financial Markets Association (SIFMA) holds a New York–based technology and data conference. Hardware, software, data, communication, and even furniture vendors display their wares over three days. This is a great opportunity to see many of the various products available. Get more information at http://www.sifma.org.

Other Information Sources

The options exchanges and the Options Clearing Corp. (OCC) provide information about stock splits, indices, volume, open interest, option calendars, and other valuable resources through their respective websites. You'll also find white papers on strategies and products, some tax information, and even videos about the market and derivative products. Appendix A lists industry websites.

After completing the original manuscript for this book, I decided to publish and make available certain tools and resources that I have developed over time, as well as a current listing of available services. Please visit www.increasingalpha.com for more information on these products.

Information Sources

Increasing Alpha	www.increasingalpha.com	Complement and updates to this book.
Bloomberg	www.bloomberg.com	News, quotes, charts
Chicago Board Options Exchange	www.cboe.com	Options information, data
International Securities Exchange	www.ise.com	Options information, data
Investors Business Daily	www.investors.com	Newspaper, charts, chart books
iVolatility.com	www.ivolatility.com	Implied/historic volatility data, options strategies, scanners
Market Technicians Association	www.mta.org	Technical analysis members
MetaStock	www.metastock.com	Charts, data
NASDAQ Market	www.nasdaq.com	Options information, data
New York Stock Exchange	www.nyse.com	Options information, data
Options Clearing Corp.	www.the-occ.com	Options information, data, options education

Quodd Financial Services	www.quodd.com	News, quotes, charts
StockCharts.com	www.stockcharts.com	Charting and data
Thomson Reuters	www.thomsonreuters.com	News, quotes, charts, data
Track Data Corp.	www.trackdata.com	News, quotes, charts, options scanners

Find an updated list and other tools at www.the-strategist.com.

Index